5 Steps to CREATING MONEY:
How to Manifest Abundance and Prosperity in Your Life

by
Dr. Alicia Holland

No parts of this book may be used or reproduced by any means, graphic, electronic, or mechanical, including photocopying, recording, taping, or by any information storage retrieval system without the written permission of the author except in this case of brief quotations embodied in critical articles and reviews.

This book may be ordered through booksellers or by contacting:

Realistic Measures & Consulting, LLC
11010 S 51st Street Unit 51572
Phoenix, Arizona 85044
www.realisticmeasures.com
323-391-6716

Because of the dynamic nature of the Internet, any web addresses or links contained in this book may have changed since publication and may no longer be valid. The views expressed in this work are solely those of the author and do not necessarily reflect the views of the publisher, and the publisher hereby disclaims any responsibility for them.

This is a work of fiction. Names, characters, businesses, places, events, and incidents are either the products of the author's imagination or used in a fictitious manner. Any resemblance to actual persons, living or dead, or actual events is purely coincidental.

FIVE STEPS TO CREATING MONEY:
How to Manifest Abundance and Prosperity in Your Life

Copyright © 2020 Dr. Alicia Holland, EdD. All Rights Reserved.

ISBN-13: 978-1944346867

Dedication

This book is dedicated to all the courageous beings who are stepping out on faith to realize their true potential in becoming a self-actualized being to utilize all of your God-Given Talents. You are never alone on this spiritual journey. Know that you are loved, you are valued, and you are competent.

Acknowledgements

I cannot say this enough, but I must give glory to God and the Archangels for helping me realize my potential and purpose in life. It was He whom brought Millicent together to manifest this project. There are truly no words to express my gratitude as each of you are truly a blessing.

I also want to thank Surendra Gupta for his creativity in formatting and designing our book. You are amazing!

About the Author

Intuitive Life Coach for the Alise Spiritual Healing & Wellness Center and Host of *The Alise Intuition Radio Show*, Dr. Alicia "Alise" Holland shares her journey from poverty to abundance, outlining steps to help you claim your own divine inheritance to serve humanity in all areas of your life—while creating a legacy for others to follow.

In the 2010's, Dr. Alise suffered a blow to the nose that changed the course of her life forever. It wasn't until she was choked after having a major surgery that she left her marriage for good. She was determined to break the generational cycle, lack mentality, and negative patterns that were holding her back from her destiny. Today, she's on her journey of becoming a Clinical Psychologist and serve humanity as an ordained Interfaith Minister, author of 40+ books, international speaker, online college professor, serial entrepreneur, thought leader, talk show personality, and is living her best life as she saw in her spiritual visions and dreams.

In *"Five Steps to Creating Money: How to Manifest Abundance and Prosperity in Your Life"*, this international expert in the field of intuition, spirituality, and intuitive life coaching shares her secrets and blueprint to designing a life that honors your authentic self in every area of your life. Dr. Alise identifies her framework—DAMNU—Discover, Acknowledge, Manifest, Navigate, Utilize—to help you connect to your intuition, tap into your creative genius, and claim your divine birthright to your inheritance. "Five Steps to Creating Money: How to Manifest Abundance and Prosperity in Your Life" offers a plethora of life lessons, actionable plans, affirmations, prayers, real-life examples, and an opportunity to connect with Dr. Alise through her mobile app for further assistance, exclusive content, and so much more.

You owe it to yourself to know who you are and why you are here so you can attract abundance and create money that will allow you to thrive and serve the world according to your divine birth plan. Remember, You are Loved, Valued, and Competent!

Table of Contents

Dedication 3
Acknowledgements 4
About the Author 5

STEP 1: Discover Your Life Purpose 9
Chapter 1: Who Are You? 10
Chapter 2: Why Are You Here? 18

STEP 2: Acknowledge that Work Must Be Done 23
Chapter 3: Reconciling Your Past 24
Chapter 4: Identifying Your Self-Worth 34
Chapter 5: Transforming Your Beliefs about
               Money and Abundance 42

STEP 3: Manifest Daily 59

Chapter 6: Manifesting What You Want 60

Chapter 7: Connecting with the Archangels
of Abundance..70

Chapter 8: Using Your Intuition and Positive
Affirmations to Manifest.................................. 79

STEP 4: Navigate the Opportunities 89

Chapter 9: What is Success? 90

Chapter 10: Diversifying Your Income Potential................ 97

STEP 5: Utilize Your God-Given Talents 109

Chapter 11: Honoring Your Value and Worth 110

Chapter 12: Having Money 117

Class Tours and Conferences 147

Notes 148

Step 1: Discover Your Life Purpose

Chapter 1:
Who Are You?

In this chapter, you will:
- Learn why you are so important.
- Learn what born identity is and why you need to know about yours.
- Describe how your spiritual gifts show up in your work.
- Assess your spiritual gifts to help you determine the type of intuition in which you have.

You Are More Than Enough

Who are you? This is a question that you will need to answer and do it honestly. Often, we think that we know who we are because we associate it with what we do or what people tell us about ourselves. The truth is this question is associated with your spiritual being. It has nothing to do with titles, degrees, social status, and whatever you have been told. Who you are is your divine identity and part of your makeup as your soul self. One of the truths that you must come to terms with is that every human being is a spiritual being. You may be religious, spiritual, or not, but you do have a home address somewhere in the spiritual realm.

Why Is It Important to Understand Your Born Identity?

Being Robbed of Your Creative Genius

One reason why it is important to understand your born identity is the world is being robbed of your creative genius. When you are not operating in your true birth identity, you are basically cheating the World. You may be the person who is destined to write that book, start that business, speak truth to the masses, be the Merchant of Hope in your generational family tree, or whatever God has ordained for your life purpose. After all, your sole reason for coming to Earth from the Spiritual Plane is to learn, grow, and share so that you can help others (and yourself) move along on your spiritual journey.

Exercising Your Divine Birth Right

Another reason why it is important to understand your born identity is it is your divine birth right. You are designed to be a Co-Creator with God and you get to do that by connecting to your intuition so that you can live a bold life in an authentic fashion that you will not have to apologize to anyone for that matter. It's about you getting with God's program on what you need to do for your life so that people will respect you. I have yet to see anyone who was living out their life purpose have a slew of haters. Of course, you will see envy and jealousy lurk around, but it has never stopped their grind or impact on the World…and it shouldn't. It's their divine birth right to live on their own terms as they co-create with God.

Your Spiritual Gifts Show up in Your Work

Since you are a spiritual being, you were designed with special gifts and talents. As you are thinking about building your brand, your spiritual gifts and talents will play a major role. For instance, imagine that you were born with the gifts of prophecy, teaching, wisdom, and knowledge. These spiritual gifts may show up in your work in the form of teaching, mentoring, life coaching, or spiritual advising. That's what your career path would entail and that's how you would look for opportunities that allow you to serve humanity with both your spiritual gifts and talents.

Being in the Right Place at the Right Time

Did you know that your spiritual gifts show up in your talents? Yes, they show up by helping you be in the right place at the right time. I have learned that you never know who you are dealing with in the public. A lot of well-respected individuals are amongst you in your community and you may not even know it. I have recognized that it is not always what you know, but who you know that can take you places. There is no coincidence when you meet people. At some point before we all got here on this Earth, there was an agreement to make that divine appointment and cross paths at that particular time.

Shining through Your Work

Another way that your spiritual gifts show up in your talents is through your work. By having the right job and the right types of education, it can catapult you into a position that allows you to take opportunities that will help your career move forward and just allow you to connect and serve humanity in a deeper way. It's not always about having a degree because many of the fabulous people and creative geniuses of our lifetime and who have come before us did not have a degree. They had great intuition, character, and walked by faith and not by sight. So, it is important to make sure that you are applying to the right jobs that will get you the skillset that can complement your spiritual gifts for your divine life purpose. In this lifetime, you may have over 10 plus jobs because we are living in times where technology is making a lot of jobs become obsolete and taking us into the digital world.

Connecting with the Right People

Another way that your spiritual gifts show up in your talents is by connecting with the right people. As I said earlier, there is no coincidence when you meet people. At some point before we all got here on this Earth, there was an agreement to make that divine appointment and cross paths at that particular time. You can look at this from a professional or personal perspective. You will find people from your soul groups who you click with and you may end up being that dedicated tribe towards your life purpose and each of these people have the resources to support you whether it is in time, energy, or money. As it relates to professional and entrepreneurship, you may find the right people to hire in your business to help meet the learning organization's goals. If you are connected to your intuition, then you will be able to identify these people as they come to interview for the positions that are made available. You will know them by their fruits and how they are committed to the vision and mission statement. It will show up in their work and you will see their true intentions because they are involved in work that is aligned to their authentic self.

Shining through Feedback and Compliments

Another way that your spiritual gifts show up in your talents is through your work. You may be able to see this when your clients whether you are employee or business owner begin to start complimenting you on your work. If you are a business owner, then you want to capture these rave reviews in your work so that you can continue to get your shine on. In the Age of the Internet, that's the first place that people check in to see more about you. Therefore, it is in your best interest to get your work in front of your target audience and it looks very good for your business or career when you have other people experiencing your product or service and leaving authentic reviews about your work.

Assessing Your Spiritual Gifts and Life Purpose

Before we go any further, let's look at some spiritual gifts that spiritual beings are gifted with no matter one's life experiences. Let's look at these spiritual gifts below.

Leadership	Teaching	Faith
• administration • discernment • hospitality • giving • service	• pastor • evangelism • apostle • knowledge • helping • wisdom	• prophecy • exhortation • miracles • healing • tongues • mercy

Now, it's time for you to assess your own spiritual gifts and reflect upon your life purpose.

1. Take a few minutes and reflect, what are your spiritual gifts?

   _____
   _____
   _____
   _____
   _____

2. How do they show up in your life, both personally and professionally?

   _____
   _____
   _____
   _____
   _____

3. What types of knowledge do you possess that can be of value to others? Please be very specific.

   _____
   _____
   _____
   _____
   _____

4. How would you describe yourself?

   _____
   _____
   _____
   _____
   _____

Chapter 2:
Why Are You Here?

In this chapter, you will:
- Learn why you are here on Earth at this time.
- Describe the characteristics of a self-actualized person.
- Describe the purpose of moving to a higher path.
- Identify your life's work.

Why are you here?

You are here to carry out your life purpose. You owe it to yourself to find out what that is. You may learn about this through relationships, including work. Your unique selling point is your Spirit. There will be some people who are afraid of your light. When you think about it, light cannot exist without darkness. We all have a dark and light side and it is up to us to choose to identify with the light. So, on that note, are you ready to let your light shine? Of course, you are.

Otherwise, you wouldn't be reading this book to learn more about how to create money and manifest your dreams into reality.

Characteristics of a Self-Actualized Person

Self-actualization implies that you have attained your full potential in life. While some people can attest to achieving it, most people are busy trying to survive and are unable to reach the optimum level in life. A self-actualized person desires to be the best they can be. Therefore, you want to achieve your goals and realize your full potential. Neither do you sacrifice your potential for the sake of others; instead, you use your power to serve others. It has everything to do with being the best you can be while being mindful of your social surroundings. You go out and attain your best with no fear and use your skills to better those around you, as well. There are characteristics of self-actualized people, and here is a look at a few of them.

- o They have had a peak experience whereby things went as they hoped to make them feel powerful and in control of their lives. Such an experience leaves one feeling reenergized and with limitless enthusiasm to pursue their dreams.
- o They accept themselves the way they are and extend the same grace to others. They have no inhibitions and will go ahead to enjoy life without any guilty feelings

whatsoever. It is not what other people think but what they think of themselves that matters.
o They take life as it comes and are not scared of what might happen their way. Tackling issues realistically, they use logic when dealing with problems that come their way.
o Self-actualized people are excellent problem solvers and like to use this skill to help situations, even those involving other people.
o They are open to new ideas and do not necessarily conform to what is expected of them. Their ideas and thoughts often reveal their impulsive nature viewed as unconventional by some people, but those ideas and thoughts work.

These are just some of the characteristics that are consistent with individuals who are conscious about their life purpose as they travel on their spiritual path towards their destiny.

The Purpose of Moving to a Higher Path

Perhaps you feel as if you are not living up to your full potential. You deserve better but have no idea how to get hold of it. Did you know that you walk your highest path when you are living true to yourself? When your most in-depth part of consciousness takes charge, you are living your higher path. Your soul consciousness allows you to perceive your connection to the universe, allowing you to walk your highest path.

You can experience life at the highest expression of your soul to be able to increase your consciousness level.

Below are several steps you can take to find your higher path:

Step #1 — Stand up for what you truly desire and feel without fear of judgment, or minding what other people think or say. This honors your soul while respecting yourself in the most compassionate level. Take responsibility for your needs without the need to hide the fact.

Step #2 — Follow your passion and use your talents. You want them to not only be a blessing to you but also other people in your life. You realize that abundance is needed to help motivate the flow of your life. It is important to know what is meant for you will find you. Therefore, do not hesitate to say no to what does not measure up to your expectations.

Step #3 — Take Risks. While it is good to be cautious, but at times, you have to take risks.
At times you have to take risks so you can reap big rewards; therefore, do not be too cautious about letting things pass you by. As long as you take responsibility for your decisions and are committed to them, you can go through the risks.

These three steps will help you continue to stay focused on serving others, but you are doing it from your authentic self, which will result in more spiritual growth. Each role that you play in life allows you to experience spiritual growth. So, if you are changing careers, jobs, friends, or relationships, then look at it as spiritual growth. There's something else that is important and needed on your life's path and it's divine timing to move forward to a new chapter in your life.

Identifying Your Life's Work

Did You know that your life's work will be your legacy? Your life's work will last you a lifetime, but it may look different in each stage of your life. For example, you may have decided to start teaching or tutoring and later end up coaching others in their life, just like me. Think about it, the Spirit will give you what you can handle and what you need at the spiritual level in which you are so that you can continue to grow, and impact others as planned according to your life plan. Everybody has a life plan and I encourage you to find out yours. That's where I can come in to help you. If this is something that interests you, then reach out to me using the contact information at the back of the book. Take a few moments, reflect upon these questions.

1. What do you think your life purpose is?

   _____
   _____
   _____
   _____
   _____

2. How will you leverage your knowledge to build a brand around your business?

   _____
   _____
   _____
   _____
   _____

These are two questions that can get you started with delving deep into your life purpose as the Spirit guides you.

Step 2: Acknowledge that Work Must Be Done

Chapter 3:
Reconciling Your Past

In this chapter, you will:
- Identify the purpose of being honest with yourself about your past.
- Describe why respecting the past and detachment are important.
- Explain the importance of removing clutter from your life.
- Describe why forgiveness about the past and your money habits are important.
- Explain why keeping your business to yourself is important.

Why Being Honest with Yourself About Your Past Is Important?

The only person you must be honest with is yourself and it is important to start with reflecting on your past the way it was without adding to it or taking away from it. It is what it is so make peace with your past. Have you ever felt better about a situation when it was over? Ok, good! This is important to look at your past in the same way. It is important to understand that your past has served a very important purpose in your life and it deserves your respect. You may be saying "What!" and asking me, "Do You Know What I Had to Endure?" The reality is that everybody has a set of life lessons in which they must learn that may not be smooth sailing, but they do serve a purpose for spiritual growth. When you find yourself getting out of your past and choosing to make new decisions so that you can learn more life lessons that are in alignment with who you are now, you will see the difference. Another reality check is that you can't change the past, even if you tried to. So, why spend so much of your energy trying to rationalize and stay in the past when you can use that energy to create new experiences. Sometimes, by associating yourself with the past, it can hold you down and keep you from moving forward and blocking your abundance flow. So, this is the first step in reconciling your past because it does need to be respected.

Why Detachment from Your Past Is Important?

Detachment from your past is important because making rational decisions at times involves removing yourself from the situation to be able to weigh it impartially. In other words, to really see what in the world is going on. This gives you an opportunity to not base situations that occurred in the past on your moods, but instead, keep clear focus so you can see available opportunities and most importantly, how far you have come in life.

Did you know the way you react to situations makes all the difference in your next move? Sure, there'll be disappointments in life, and instead of dwelling on them, you should channel your energy to more constructive things. Emotional detachment keeps you positive and without negative emotions or thoughts. When you are emotionally stable and detached, it allows you to see what happens around you for what it is, so it does not affect you. This is a skill that you will have to continue to practice and it gets even harder when it is dealing with family and friends. However, you still need to have healthy boundaries set for them as well. Emotional detachment will stop you from taking things personally. When you face tumultuous times, you'll be able to rise above them and handle situations in the right manner.

Please keep in mind that there will be times when you face criticism from those around you, but let it strengthen you. When you dwell on such negativity, then it can delay your vision and ultimately affect your abundance flow. You must have a good understanding of yourself and know in your heart that your position with God has not changed. God still sees you as the beautiful creation and you are loved, valued, and competent in his eyes. When searching for prosperity and abundance, you need to learn how to let go of things that have no meaning and focus on those that do, including the people who are honest with you and celebrate you. At the end of the day, you owe it to yourself to make independent decisions that will honor and respect you.

The Importance of Removing Clutter from Your Life

You need to continuously remove everything in your life that does not serve you any longer. This is an effective way for you to start manifesting abundance in your life. Get rid of things you don't need to make room for new ones in all areas of your life. When you remove things you no longer use in your home, you make room to acquire things you need. Most people have things they no longer need all over their house, making the place disorderly. You can put up a garage sale to get rid of clutter or even give them away to people who need them. The same goes for your office as well. For instance, you might find outdated equipment sitting in the office, taking up unnecessary space. Having stuff scattered all over the place can even clutter your mind as well; therefore, ensure you do not have unnecessary items lying around. You do not want to stress yourself with things that have no space in your life anymore. Clutter can be stressful and can influence your decision making because you are living around it. It can distract you and take away joy from your life if left that way. You don't want that!

You'll have a more organized life if you are clutter-free and have a more pleasing space to enjoy productivity. If you find that this is a challenge, then begin small and work to getting rid of more stuff you do not need over time. Most areas of your life need decluttering, including relationships that might be overwhelming as well as spaces around you. It is 100% okay to give yourself the permission to remove whatever necessary in your life that is blocking your energy to manifest new opportunities in all areas of your life. Now, let's take it a step further and focus on forgiving yourself about your past money habits.

Forgiving Yourself About Your Past Money Habits

You may have had bad money habits. It might be something you still struggle with even now. No matter the case, it's important for you to forgive yourself and forge ahead. Your mistakes do not define you; therefore, let go of them.

Below are three reasons why you need to forgive yourself about your bad money habits:

Accept and Live Past the Mistake	Learn the Life Lessons	Plan Your Next Financial Move

Accept and Live Past the Mistake

The first reason why you need to forgive yourself about your bad money habits is because you cannot change what you did in the past. It won't help for you to dwell on the past with thoughts of what you did wrong. You need to let it go, so you do not continue to focus on the issue wasting even more time. Quit beating yourself up over a wrong decision that you made because it takes up energy you could use planning your next move. You need to forgive yourself for making mistakes regarding your finances. If you get past your money mistakes then you will have a healthy attitude to spur you on to success. Learn from your mistakes and determine to do better next time. You can rebuild a solid foundation that can be even firmer than before because you have made a decision to accept that you made a bad financial move and now it's time to focus on how to move past the mistake.

Learn the Life Lessons

The second reason why you need to forgive yourself about your bad money habits is to learn the life lessons associated with your money. It is important to take time to go over what you did wrong so you can avoid the same behavior in the future. It may help to visualize how you plan on budgeting your money. Let's get to the root cause of your relationship to money. As you answer the following questions, please be honest with yourself:

1. What did my parents teach me about money?

   _____
   _____
   _____
   _____
   _____

2. What has been my relationship with money in the past?

3. Do you respect money? Do you view it as a tool? Why or why not?

4. What is your own definition of 'having money'? What does this look like to you?

5. What is my relationship with money now?

6. How do I want my relationship with money to look in the future?

_____
_____
_____
_____

As you continue to be honest with yourself about your money habits, continue to humble yourself and really get to the bottom of the root causes of these financial patterns instead of blaming yourself. When you are ready, it's time to plan your next financial move.

Plan Your Next Financial Move

The last reason why you need to forgive yourself about your bad money habits is to plan your next financial move. Are you on the right path financially? If you realize you are off track in your finances, it is time to reorganize them. Your next financial move is to create a personal finance system that includes a budget. I talk more about this in Chapter 12.

Keeping Your Business to Yourself

You probably know it is better to keep your business to yourself. Like the rest of your life, you should keep it that way if you can. On next page, I share three reasons why you should keep your business to yourself.

1) *You stay in control of your destiny.* Since you want the best for your business, you'll be able to make the best decisions concerning it opposed to having someone else involved in your business. Sometimes, people who say that they are happy for you is not happy for you. They may try to keep you from moving forward by causing doubt with your thinking process. A lot of people might appear to be friends, but few of them are not beneficial to your business in the end. However, at some point, you will need to involve other people but you want to do so when you have your own abundance flow and spiritual energy in alignment with your purpose to attract the type of energy that can help everyone succeed.

2) *You are not accountable to anyone but God and Yourself.* It is so important to create a work-life balance so that you can live your life in divine order. You get to set your priorities, and it allows you to spend time on the principal purpose of life. When you put God first, your spouse, your family, and everything else then you will naturally see the flow of your abundance impacted positively.

3) *You take your own risk.* You learn as you grow and do not have to deal with negativity from other people. The decisions you make are entirely your own; therefore, you can deal with the results by yourself as well. People can steal your attention, so you no longer focus on your business if you let them.

Now, that you have focused on reconciling your past, looking at the importance of removing clutter, and keeping your business to yourself. It's time to focus on you and your personal power. Let's start with identifying your self-worth.

Chapter 4:
Identifying Your Self-Worth

In this chapter, you will:
- Identify what is self-worth.
- Learn the importance of your self-worth.
- Describe the purpose of setting healthy boundaries.
- Assess whether you have self-worth issues to work on.

What is Self-Worth?

It took me a long time to come up with this definition through lived experiences, but I have come to learn that self-worth is how we view ourselves. This became very evident to me once I became an entrepreneur. You can look at a person's choice and determine how he or she views himself or herself. However, I have also learned that we cannot simply judge someone for what we see on the outside looking in, but we should focus on the flow of his or her heart to see if those choices are made out of love and integrity. Throughout our lifetime, each of us will find ourselves having self-worth and self-esteem issues. Often times, we see these come up in our romantic relationships, and career choices. Therefore, it's important to focus on building your self-esteem as it will affect all areas of your life resulting in you teaching people how to treat you as you interact with them.

Why is Self-Worth Important?

One of the hardest life lessons, besides forgiveness, is to learn how to love oneself the way that God has created you. Did you know that your self-worth is tied to how you show up in the world in business, love, and overall? Well, I am here to tell you that it is because when you feel good on the inside it shows on the outside. Your self-worth is your G-Code. In other words, people get to know your heart through your actions so your intentions are on display and people will see it one way or another as they interact with you. It does not matter what your parents did, what your grandparents did, what your siblings did, because you are your own person. You were born with your own identity and you owe it to yourself to know what that is to better help you realize that you are the most prized possession in God's eyes. There is nothing that you can do to change that because your position with God has not changed. So, don't let anyone tell you that you are not worth anything. For example, when that particular job you have had for x about of years has been cut, it is important to know that your value was not diminished. You learned the skillsets and knowledge that you needed to move forward on your life purpose. Another example is when that relationship did not work out, it was for your highest good. Remember, you are God's most prized possession and the Spirit is not going to allow you to keep going through situations that will keep you from your life purpose. Now, if you *choose* to stay in that kind of connection, then that is your free will choice. It is important to know that the Universe always offer an opportunity for you to get out, but it goes back to you making the decision for yourself and knowing your self-worth. In other words, God wants to know if you are going to do what is best for the love of you and how you are going to honor yourself. A third example is when you are passed over for a position that you are more than qualified to assume the responsibilities. One thing that I have learned is that rejection is protection. There was something about that position that was not for your highest good. You may not see it right away, but rest assured, God will show you why that position was not ordained for you. If you experience this, it just means that something better is in store for you and it will be in alignment with your authentic self and what your heart truly desires. After all, at the end of the day, when you leave one job, your spiritual gifts and talents go with you. You will be in a better position to either accept or reject the next opportunity so choose wisely.

The Importance of Setting Boundaries

Setting healthy boundaries is one of the best gifts that you can give yourself and others. You are teaching people that you honor, respect, and value yourself. This is something that money cannot buy, or anyone can steal away from you because it is coming from the inside of you. The purpose of setting healthy boundaries is so that you can operate in a way that makes you feel good about yourself. On the flip side of that, you can help others feel good about interacting with you as you work with them or interact with them. This will allow every person involved learn how he or she needs to interact with you to have a positive experience. Otherwise, if you do not set healthy boundaries with others, then you give them permission to treat you how they want to do so. It's important to note that people are not going to treat you how you *think* you need to be treated, but they will treat you according to their own lived experiences. Therefore, it's important to understand that people may do things from their subconscious and may not be aware of their own actions because they have unresolved emotional trauma and issues that may have stemmed from their childhood or a series of unfortunate events that have taught them how to protect themselves. You do not want others to use you as their source in which they can dump all their emotional issues on you. It's not your place to deal with their emotional issues so that's the purpose of setting healthy boundaries. The biggest thing that I have learned is that it is okay to be honest with yourself about the issues that you need to work through. After all, we are not perfect, and we will have flaws that we will need to work on throughout our lifetime. However, it's important to know that you have free will choice to determine which life lessons that you want to deal with to elevate your own spiritual growth. On that note, let's take a quick quiz to see if you are dealing with self-worth issues.

Assessing Your Self-Worth

The number one thing about making changes is being honest with yourself. Don't worry, if you are reading this book, then your soul is calling you to really look deep within and be honest with yourself so that you can make the necessary changes in which your heart truly desires. Before you can begin to create money the way that your soul wants to express itself, you will need to answer a few questions so you can become aware of what it is that you really want and what are the insights in which you need to know to get there.

Please write down your answers to the following questions.

1. What is your own definition of self-worth?

_____
_____
_____
_____

2. What type of boundaries, if any, do you currently have in place with family, friends, coworkers, colleagues, and in your love life?

_____
_____
_____
_____
_____

3. How would you describe how others treat you in love?

_____
_____
_____
_____
_____

4. How would you describe how others treat you at work?

_____
_____
_____
_____
_____

5. What are five adjectives that you would use to describe yourself? Why?

6. What are five adjectives that you think others would use to describe you? Why?

7. How do you value yourself? What does that look like?

8. How do you allow others to value you? Is it in alignment with who you are? Why or why not?

_____
_____
_____
_____
_____

As you continue to be honest with yourself about how you value yourself and allow others to interact with you, it will help you see what you need to change so that you can improve your energy flow to attract more abundance in all areas of your life. When you are healthy and happy on the inside, then it shows up in everything that you do. You become radiant and everyone sees that glow as they interact with you.

Now let's focus on transforming your beliefs about money and abundance in the next chapter.

Chapter 5:

Transforming Your Beliefs about Money and Abundance

In this chapter, you will:
- Identify your own belief system about money and abundance.
- Describe why transforming your beliefs are key.
- Learn strategies on how to release outdated thoughts.
- Assessing your debt emotionally.
- Learn strategies to create a new relationship with money.

- Learn the spiritual laws associated with money and abundance.
- Identify personal values associated with money and abundance.

What is Your Belief System About Money and Abundance?

The number one thing about making changes is being honest with yourself. Don't worry, if you are reading this book, then your soul is calling you to really look deep within and be honest with yourself so that you can make the necessary changes in which your heart truly desires. Before you can begin to create money the way that your soul wants to express itself, you will need to answer a few questions so you can become aware of what it is that you really want.

Please write down your answers to the following questions:

1. What are your beliefs about money and abundance?

_____
_____
_____
_____
_____

2. What were you told about money and abundance in your childhood?

_____
_____
_____
_____
_____

3. Did you see a lot of money and abundance when you were growing up? How did that look in your life?

_____
_____
_____
_____
_____

4. Do you believe that you can have money and abundance? Why or why not?

_____
_____
_____
_____
_____

As you continue to be honest with yourself about your early opportunities with money and abundance, you will begin the process of helping you get a grasp of what you really believe about money and abundance. Let's look at why transforming your beliefs are important to create money and attract abundance.

Why Transforming Your Beliefs Are Key?

Each of us has his or her own set of beliefs that shape our lives. It not only affects our view of ourselves but of others as well and the entire world too. Our emotions and actions get influenced by it too. As a result, beliefs also determine how happy and prosperous we are. You need to discover the core of your belief to be able to facilitate change in your behavior and emotions. What other people envision of you should not chart the path of your life, but it is the thoughts you have of yourself. In this regard, belief is critical in the direction your life will take. Below are three reasons why transforming your beliefs are key and should be your priority to help enhance your life.

Change Beliefs, Get Results	Limiting Beliefs Hold You Back	Beliefs Impact Your Life
When you change your beliefs, you will also change your thoughts and that's when you will begin to see real change.	When you hold on to a belief, it keeps you from moving forward and seeing a new way of doing things for your highest good.	Whatever you belief in, it will show up in your actions and will ultimately shape the course of your destiny and level of your success because you will serve your beliefs.

Beliefs are an integral part of you, and a change from negative to positive ones can make a whole lot of difference for you. Let these three reasons marinate to help you recognize the need for a change of beliefs to help you get where you want to be in life.

Releasing Outdating Thoughts for Your Highest Good

Letting go of outdated thoughts involves embracing new ideas and not being stuck on the old. If you find yourself unable to let go of old ideas, you might be curtailing any improvements in your life. Even then, you will need to respect other people's way of life and traditions. There are some strategies that can help you release outdated thoughts so that you can make room to cater to the new thoughts that the Spirit is giving you through your intuition. Therefore, it's important that you pay close attention to your surroundings and any signs in which you may be getting as the Angels and Spirit will communicate with you new ideas on how to help you solve problems or just move forward towards your life purpose. You do this by connecting to your intuition daily.

On the next page there are some strategies that can help you release outdated thoughts so that you can make room to cater to the new thoughts that the Spirit is giving you through your intuition.

Strategy #1 — Make time each day to be able to think over any thoughts that might be hindering progress. Anything that limits you is worth dropping, and you need time to identify such thoughts. Have a picture of the way things will be if you release outdated thoughts.

Strategy #2 — Embrace new thoughts. Do not be afraid to embrace a new way of thinking as it could lead to a new way of life. Old thoughts can, at times, seem like chains that limit your potential. After embracing new thoughts, you should go ahead and implement them.

Strategy #3 — Have positive affirmations. Thoughts such as `I can" `I will" send the right message to your brain, which then adapts your thought patterns. Your affirmations should be strong enough to get your mind moving in the right direction for success.

Strategy #4 — Do not dwell on past mistakes. This only waste time you could use making positive actions towards success. Learn from them and let go of thoughts of doing things the same way and gain new insight on the way of doing things.

When you release old thoughts, you make room for new ones; You allow your mind to explore new ideas that could end up to a new break in life. Your thoughts determine the kind of life you lead, therefore do not get stuck on old thoughts that have been passed by time. God is trying to move you forward so work with the Universe on moving further on your life path to what destiny has for you.

Assessing Your Debt Emotionally

Everybody has debt whether it is karmic or financial. With the right motivation, you can be able to get out of financial debt. You, however, need to determine your debt emotionally to be able to find ways of getting out of it. Accept the predicament, but do not let it weigh you down. Debt can cause health problems, including depression; therefore, it has emotional effects on a person. Be honest about the state of things. There can be nothing worse than for you to pretend like you are not in debt. Instead, you should face up to the fact and find ways of getting out of it. At the end of the day, you need to understand why you got in debt in the first place. So, set aside some time to look a bit closer at your debt.

EXERCISE: Getting to the Root of My Debt

Take the time out and gather your bills and be honest with yourself as you look at each one. When you look at each bill, reflect on why you got the debt. What is the backstory of it? What was going on at that time that caused you to get into that specific debt? Jot down any thoughts, insights, that come to mind.

Please write down your answers to the following questions.

1. What did you learn about the emotions associated with your debt?

2. What are your plans about these debts to release these emotions associated with it?

_____
_____
_____
_____
_____

Your debt does not define you. You are not necessarily a bad person and should not dwell on past mistakes. Instead, understand the reason you got into debt and evade it as much as you can. Your efforts to work yourself out of debt will eventually pay off if you do not allow yourself to get bogged down with it. By paying off your debts when you can, this can psychologically set you on the right track because it will provide hope for you to get over it. Where there is hope, anxiety and depression will have no room in mind. You need all of your energy so that you can create a new relationship with your money and how you view debt as there is a huge difference between bad debt and good debt because your emotions are associated with each type of debt.

Creating a New Financial Relationship History with Money

After you have taken some time to look at your debt from an emotional stance, now it's time to see what you can do to continue to create a new financial relationship history with money. If you are still paying off debt, then these strategies become even more important as you consistently manifest opportunities to have more experience with money. Below are some strategies that can help you better understand your relationship with money:

Strategy #1: Reflect on Past Thoughts About Money

Think of the positive thoughts you had about money growing up as well as the less pleasant ones. There are lessons to learn from your history with money that can help you create a new relationship with your finances.

Strategy #2: Reflect on Your Family's Money Story

What's your family story? Learn of the relationship of your family members with money. There's a lot to learn from them, including mistakes you can avoid in your financial decisions. You might need to speak to family members to find out their stories, and it will help you form better decisions regarding money. If you find yourself in a situation with family members who are secretive about their money habits, then that is a red flag and should be noted as part of the family's money story because there's a deeper emotional connection to that behavior. In time, the Spirit will show you and you will be able to make a connection of the family's history with money. All you must do is ask God and the Angels to show you and it will be done.

Strategy #3: Reflect on Your Relationship with Money

It has to do with our sense of self and serves as a deeper understanding of ourselves. The way you behave around money tells a lot about who you are. If you know this, you'll be able to improve the way you function financially. Your money spending patterns can reveal a lot about what is going on with you.

Strategy #4: Get a Financial Mentor

Get yourself a mentor in financial matters. There's no telling what a significant influence someone who's been there and gone through the process can add to your experience. Find someone with evidence of making the right money decisions and learn a lesson or two from them. It helps if you know you can realize success by learning from someone who has made it already or have experience repeating the same money mistakes.

Spiritual Laws Associated with Money and Abundance

We have a set of spiritual laws that are associated with every aspect of your life. Did you know that there are spiritual laws associated with money and abundance? Yes, there are, and we are going to take a closer look at them so that you can have better understanding of how they apply in your financial life.

Spiritual Laws of Money

It is difficult to separate money from spirituality, no doubt. Religion requires money to run; therefore, it is essential to embrace its role. The concept that money is evil needs to get discarded, to begin with. Understand that there's nothing evil about money as it all depends on its use. It's for the *love* of money that gets people into trouble because they are not able to separate their ego or desire of getting money by any means necessary. *This* is one of the Spiritual laws you need to embrace. Recognize it as an instrument to get things done and not necessarily good or bad. Open your mind to the possibilities of making money. Spirituality broadcasts positive virtues in plenty, and you should embrace the same regarding money. Drop the scarcity mentality and seek opportunities to make money. The fact that you have money in your possession should not be cause for guilt feelings. If you make it through with just a little bit of money, there should be no reason for you to harbor guilt feelings. It's important to focus on the life lessons in which you are learning in this season of your life. It's making you stronger. Even though spiritually, you will not be able to take money with you when you die. The only thing that you have is your soul that goes on with you in the afterlife.

You need ideas to get rich. If you have an idea that could generate money when put into use, then be sure to make use of it. You don't necessarily have to have money to make more as with an idea you can achieve the same. Therefore, it is important for you to get in touch with your spiritual gifts and talents that will help you with your life purpose.

Be sure to make use of money to get you where you want to be, but do not make it your sole objective for living. Money alone will not make you happy therefore embrace spiritualism to be able to understand yourself better.

Attainment of money is gradual, just like spiritualism. Do not expect to attain your money goals at the snap of a finger. Embrace the process that goes with it and do not seek shortcuts to get it. And just as there should be no competition in spiritualism so too should there be none where the money is concerned. It is an individual journey, after all.

Spiritual Laws of Abundance

What are the spiritual laws of Abundance? When it comes to the spiritual laws of abundance, it is important to know that an even energetic exchange must occur to keep the abundance flowing like a river. Having a constant flow of positive things in life is what constitutes Abundance. Being able to embrace it depends a whole lot on you including your view of yourself and your beliefs among others. You owe it to yourself to remove anything that stands in the way of enjoying Abundance. Love, for instance. You can choose to embrace love or close your heart to it. There are many reasons you might do that, but none of them justifies you to block the flow of love.

Abundance is about taking advantage of the flow of life so you can have an enjoyable one. Whatever you desire in life, you should give off in Abundance to be able to attract it back to you — friendship, for instance. You attract more friends if you are friendly to other people. Give off the right energy and it will come back to you. This is one of the spiritual laws of Abundance.

The measure of real success is in inner satisfaction. The spiritual law of Abundance touches all aspects of life. Accept Abundance in order to be able to receive that which you desire. The spiritual law of Abundance tells us to be conscious of our needs so they can flow to us.

As has been said, there is a lot of money to be acquired on earth, and all that matters are the desire to attain it. If you set your mind on getting the wealth, you send out the energy that attracts the same. If you are willing to go by the spiritual rules to enable you to achieve money, you will no doubt get what you desire. Tap into the generosity of the universe by having the right attitude of Abundance to be able to get the money you need.

Spiritual Laws of Giving and Receiving

What are the spiritual laws of giving and receiving? One of the spiritual laws of giving and receiving is what you will come back to you. For the energy to continue, we need to keep the flow going.

These spiritual laws operate on the belief that the entire universe is on the move, and for one to receive, they too must give continuously. Simply put, receiving and giving makeup two diverse channels of similar energy flow.

Ceasing to either receive or give causes the powerful energy to be cut off from our lives. We must make sure that we keep it flowing. For example, in the area of love, if you are involved in a relationship where you are the one putting out all of the energy, then there is an unbalanced flow of energy that is radiating throughout that relationship which will cause a feeling of not being valued to come upon you. On the other hand, if you are the one that is constantly taking from your partner or others and never giving in return, then the energetic cycle cannot be completed resulting in your abundance flow being impacted. That's the same concept with having energies around you that are not supportive in what you are doing in life. It's not going to help you move forward because of the negativity that is affecting your own positive energy flow. Abundance goes deeper than just money, but your happiness, joy, peace, love, and sense of self are also at stake when you are not being aware of how you are giving and receiving energy as you travel on your life's journey.

For instance, should blood stop flowing in the body, then what? It leads to clotting and coagulation. Similarly, energy can get viewed as the flow gets cut off when it becomes motionless. We are unable to get our desires to come to us since the flow has been cut off.

It is human to want to hold back from giving when running low on resources. This mainly stems from the fear we will not have enough for ourselves. It is the understanding the constant flow of energy in receiving constitutes the law of giving and receiving, nevertheless. However, do not give to receive as it loses the beauty of giving but give to give joy to the recipient of your kindness.

If you can determine to give without allowing fear of being without, you will throw open the door of joy in having it all come back to you. An in equal measure be ready to receive as well, so as to keep the energy flowing. When you open your heart to receiving, you allow the other person to experience the joy of giving and in turn, charge your heart to do the same.

Spiritual Laws of Attraction

What are the spiritual laws of attraction? The Law of attraction works for not just material prosperity but the spiritual as well. It is a flow of energy that comes from a universal source. In things, we need to be able to satisfy, the purpose of our life's abundance is the mission of our soul. Using the Law of attraction, one is able to draw abundance into life. But first, we need to have an attitude of gratefulness as everything that happens to us has a lesson in it.

One of the things that hinder the spiritual laws of attraction from taking effect in our lives is negative emotions such as fear. You cannot be a channel of positive flow if we get filled with fear, thus will not be able to attract your desires in life.

A sure way of activating the Law of attraction is by envisioning what we want to have happen in our lives. Belief has everything to do with it; therefore, it maintains a positive belief in all things. Whatever you believe of yourself, you will indeed become in the end.

For your desires to manifest, you have to be very clear about what they are. The Law of attraction gets invoked by positive affirmation, as well as the belief you will succeed.

Confidence is another essential tool of the Law of attraction. Coupled with the belief, it will lead to success in what you envision. Similar things tend to move towards each other; therefore, positive thoughts will more likely steer you to success.

When you shift your understanding and perspective regarding your relationship with the universe, you are then able to attract positive things in life. For the Law to start working for you, you must intentionally think of items you want to see in your life. If you believe that it works, you will no doubt see things turn in the direction of your desires. The next step in how to create money is to manifest daily. Let's take a closer look at what Step 3 entails.

Step 3: Manifest Daily

Chapter 6: Manifesting What You Want

In this chapter, you will:
- Identify what is manifestation.
- Learn why survival mode blocks abundance.
- Describe the importance of releasing emotional blocks.
- Learn strategies to help you manifest what you want.
- Apply manifestation strategies to your own life.
- Assess your life based upon your manifestation goals.

What is Manifestation?

Manifestation is a term used in spirituality to mean an individual's desire to attract a certain experience. A lot of people associate manifestation with the law of attraction.

It's one thing to attract what you want, but do you know how to keep it? This is where I teach people about setting positive intentions towards what they want for the right reasons. True manifestation happens when individuals attract opportunities into their lives not only because those opportunities align with their life purpose, but because they serve the highest good for all parties involved. With this approach, opportunities continue to materialize from one generation to the next. Manifestation should be a process that is not based upon ego - because ego does not radiate from divine love. Remember, divine love heals and prospers.

Let's take a look at the impact of survival mode on your flow of abundance.

Why Survival Mode Blocks Abundance?

You have likely faced financially challenging times at one time or another. This in itself may have been enough to force you into survival mode. Survival mode can happen as a result of financial insecurity, which keeps you living in uncertainty and fear of lacking. At times like this you are more likely to make bad decisions. This is the main reason why living with an active survival mode blocks abundance; it's impossible to see clearly what your next strategic move should be. Therefore, it's in your best interest to reduce debt as much as possible so that you can begin to retain earnings and learn how to set and manage a budget. We will discuss more about budgets in Chapter 12.

When living abundantly, your focus is on investing in causes that are greater than yourself. A person living in survival mode has no experience with abundant living. They live from one crisis to the next and may view abundance as a time when there is no real crisis to deal with. It is difficult for an individual to visualize abundance when living on the edge of financial crisis all the time. Survival mode blocks abundance for several reasons.

Most people resort to borrowing to make up for deficiencies in financial need. Debt is a sure block to abundance and could end up leading one further down the drain. Some people choose not to deal with the situation as it is and don't take responsibility for it. This could end up being a costly mistake, not only financially, but spiritually.

When in survival mode, it is easy to fall for all manner of magical solutions promising to help keep you afloat. The tempting solutions end up sending you further into debt, thus curtailing your hope for abundance. At the time, you can decide to bury your head in the sand and live life as if things are alright. This will most likely lead to more debt and create further distance between you and abundance.

Living in fear of not having enough money for your needs only pushes abundance further away from you. It would be best to face up to the fact that some days are bad, and to positively forge ahead in the quest for success. Choose to be responsible in your financial seasons of life.

The Importance of Releasing Emotional Blocks

Emotional blocks can stand in the way of attracting money. For you to be successful and pave the way to attract money, you need to release them. Here are strategies on how to get rid of emotional blocks standing:

- *Believe that you deserve money.* You might think that success is for other people and not you. This is a limiting belief and could interfere with attracting cash. Anyone deserves the cash, and you need to challenge yourself daily on the fact. Money is necessary to take care of basic needs so that you can do the work that will take you nearer to your life purpose, attracting both abundance and prosperity.
- *Rid yourself of money blocks.* Money is not necessarily evil; it is the wrongful use of it that could be detrimental. If this is your mindset, remind yourself that there's nothing wrong with having too much or too little of it. For every negative belief about money, replace it with a positive one. Money is a tool and it is to be used to carry out your life purpose to serve humanity. It's the flow of your heart that truly matters.
- *Reframe your mind to focus on abundance.* Instead of dwelling of how difficult it is to make money, you can choose instead to keep in mind the fact that you are capable of making cash given the right circumstances.

It's important to think about the gifts and talents that you know you are good at or what trusted people have told you that you are good at. This will help point you in the direction of where your time would be best spent in order to attract abundance.
- *Obey your intuition.* You may call it your gut feelings, but those are the feelings you get when you are just about to do something is the universe pointing you to your destiny. Ignoring them could turn out to be an expensive mistake, one you cannot afford. Be conscious of these feelings and pay heed to the direction they push you. Sometimes, your intuition can reveal novel ideas that will not only bring money to you, but help others in the World. Your intuitions are messages from God.
- *Recognize that having low expectations can also be a way to block attracting money.* Low expectations and doubt can create negative energy, blocking your access to cash. Have high expectations, and you'll be able to attract money and watch things change for the better.

Attracting money depends a lot on removing anything that standing in the way of your success. Take account of any such doubts and negativity and get rid of them. You owe it to yourself to start transforming your mindset about money. Realize that you are very deserving of the good and financial security coming your way.

Strategies to Help You Manifest What You Want

There are ways to manifest what you want. It's important to understand that you want to manifest people, places, and things in your life with positive intentions. When it comes to goals, it can be challenging to find the time to work on them. Day to day life has become quite busy, and it is natural to get drawn in the humdrum of life and overlook manifesting your goals.

Goals can take months or years to work on, and the worst that can happen is to let time go by without any action on our part. Most goals are shattered from years of neglect. Here are strategies to help you set aside time to manifest and work on goals:

- *Ensure daily progress.* Create a routine of working towards your goals even when you don't feel like it. You can set aside time each day to manifest on your goals.
- *Schedule a specific time.* This should be a time when you feel most productive. Consider waking before others to work with focus and intent. Do not wait for the time when you feel like working on your goals, but ensure you create a habit by sitting down at the same time every day.
- *Focus.* It is important to focus on doing the things that need to be done each day and to not doubt your abilities. If you focus on completing work each day and not on the overall outcome, the results will no doubt manifest soon enough. Even if it takes a great effort

to focus on the main task each day, that will be more than enough - you are learning how to manage and value your time to make progress toward your daily task list.
- *Trying to make up for lost time can be tiresome.* If you miss a day of work, you can make up for it on days when you are fully engaged and can be much more productive for a longer time than planned. Do not, however, push yourself to work to fill in for the lost time.

At the end of each day, write down the work that needs to get done the following day. Being clear and setting yourself up for achievement adds to the enthusiasm to get on with work no matter the day. Success involves approaching on your goals each day to achieve what you want.

Applying Manifestation Strategies to Your Life

You can manifest anything you want in life through the use of the right methods. Remember, the key is to make sure that your intentions are positive. Tt is the flow of your heart that truly matters. Here are five ways for you to manifest whatever it is you want in life:

- *Work at attaining your goals.* This is perhaps the most critical step that you need in order to take to manifest what you desire. There is no stopping once you have your goals in place, and you have to keep working at

achieving them. It might involve finding ways to do so, but you should not stop until you attain your desire.
- *Visualize your dreams.* If you can see whatever it is you want in your mind's eye, you can go on to achieve it. The more vivid it appears, the easier it will be for you to achieve. Add feeling to it, and you'll be able to attain what it is you desire.
- *Prepare for success.* You will need to make room for what you are hoping for. For instance, make room to receive more cash by having a bank account. By focusing on what you wish for and going a step further to prepare to receive it, you are moving toward manifesting your dream. The universe is generous and will give you whatever you want, depending on the desire you portray.
- *Have a clear mind.* If you want new ideas to take root, you have to first clear your mind. You can then focus on the important stuff and let go of the junk.
- *Write your goals down.* This serves as a blueprint to help you get what you want in life. Writing your dreams down on paper makes them real. Your subconscious mind then registers what you want, and this helps you set your goals, and ultimately achieve them.

Assessing Your Life Based on Your Manifestation Goals

As you are moving further and further along on your life path, you will need to get in the habit of assessing your life based upon the manifestation of goals and practice of gratitude as part of positive manifestation. Here are some questions that you should consider each time you see a manifestation come to pass:

1. How does it feel to see your goal materialize?

   _____
   _____
   _____
   _____
   _____

2. Are the goals that you are manifesting in alignment with who you are now? Why or why not?

   _____
   _____
   _____
   _____
   _____

3. How will you keep track of the goal(s) you have manifested?

   _____
   _____
   _____
   _____
   _____

4. What are your next steps to further this goal?

   _____
   _____
   _____
   _____
   _____

5. What are you grateful for since this goal has been achieved? Be specific.

   _____
   _____
   _____
   _____
   _____

At this point you have identified what manifestation is and why it is important to continue to release emotional blocks in your life. Additionally, you had an opportunity to learn strategies to help manifest what you want and reflect upon your life as your desires materialize. Let's move on to the next chapter on how to connect with the Archangels of Abundance.

Chapter 7: Connecting with the Archangels of Abundance

In this chapter, you will:
- Identify what is Ancestral Money.
- Describe the importance of ancestral money.
- Learn what it means to let money flow.
- Discover how to connect to the Archangels of Abundance.
- Learn spiritual practices to connect to the Archangels.

What is Ancestral Money?

Ancestral money is money that your ancestors made and perhaps left for inheritance. It would benefit you to learn a few facts regarding this type of income so that you can understand what they did right on the journey to achieving this financial success.

Your personal relationship with money could be based on how your ancestors interacted with their own finances. Patterns can be either inherited or learned from older generations. You will most likely recognize a few of them in your own actions if you look closely enough. Some inclinations you should retain while others need to be discarded. You have a choice to either continue on with these patterns or drop them altogether and alter the patterns for future generations. But first, you need to understand how your ancestors made their money and what they spent it on.

Find out from living relatives if there are family stories regarding attitudes toward money that would help you in your own financial endeavors. Consider anything your parents might have said or done to teach you about money when you were growing up. Take note of what seemed to work for them, and what didn't.

It's important to understand your family's financial attitudes and situations, and this might be different on the paternal and maternal side. By analyzing what has and hasn't worked for past generations, you can make a lucrative start of your own.

Ancestral money will help you gauge what works best in business and can be beneficial in pointing you in the right direction. The things that worked for your ancestors will work for you if you adopt their attitudes toward making money and their spending habits as well. If you discover old money patterns that are no longer relevant, you should disregard those as they can be a drain to your energy, making progress impossible.

Why is Ancestral Money Important?

Ancestral money is important because you want to make sure that you are doing your part to provide for future generations in your family. If you come from a family that has been broke for decades, centuries, or even longer, then guess what - your beliefs about money will be greatly skewed and you'll be unable to accept abundance and prosperity into your life. Coming from this type of background may mean that you will have to learn how to create money using your God-given gifts and talents.

In the event that you were born into wealth, it is incredibly important to look at the family generations to see exactly how that money was earned and how wealth was sustained over time from one generation to the next.

We have all heard about how people lose their family's wealth or how some families have risen out of poverty because of an idea, skill, or gift that they can use to their benefit. If no one in your family wants to talk about this type of history, then research as much as you can. It is your divine birthright to know about your ancestors' relationship with money so that you can either continue to participate or create your own family legacy with new beliefs, new ways to view money, and the use of positive intent to attract abundance and prosperity.

Letting Money Flow

Taking advantage of the law of attraction is a great way to make money flow in your life. You attract the things that you think about often. This is true of money in general, including obtaining it, retaining it, and sustaining it.

Positive patterns in thought can lead to success. When you let money flow, you are not afraid to spend it reasonably. You are aware of the value of money and have respect for it as well. Only give it to those who can pay it back. When making purchases, you should go for quality things even though they cost more rather than buying cheap, low-quality stuff that only takes up space and will not last long.

It is essential to save some cash for future needs that might arise. Be in the habit of positive confession where the money is concerned as your mind will get used to this and help you to achieve it. If you are always talking about how broke you are, you put a negative focus on money, and this can create a negative outcome in your finances.

One useful habit that of maintaining an outflow of finances as well as an increase in in-flow. In this way, you'll be able to attract endless opportunities by properly circulating wealth after creating it. It might mean having a different mental attitude where instead of merely surviving, you insist on living your life.

Attract the flow of money by making it through honest and proper means and also using it for real needs. Instead of hoarding money, you should put it into circulation, as this is the right way to let money flow in your life. Use what you make to allow room for you to make more of it, as long as the use is justifiable.

Connecting to the Archangels of Abundance

Did you know that God has appointed specific Angels to help you with abundance and prosperity? Abundance goes further than just financial blessings. In fact, abundance and prosperity include true, divine love that heals and prospers. This can come in the form of emotionally fulfilling work, relationships, and of course, financial abundance. As a child of God, it is your divine birthright to receive abundance at every stage of your life.

Let's take a look at the Archangels that are responsible for abundance and prosperity and their specific roles in serving humanity:

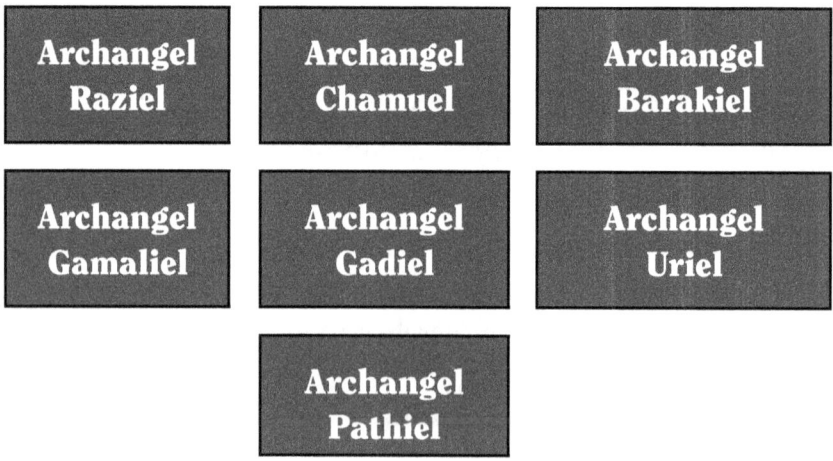

These are the Archangels in which I communicate on a regular basis because I am spiritually connected to the

Angelic Realm. Each of these Archangels have a specific unique role in serving humanity. Let's look at each of their specific functions:

Archangels of Abundance and Prosperity	Specific Functions
Archangel Raziel	Known as the Mysterious Angel who can bring abundance out of nowhere. This is the Angel to call upon when you have a dire need.
Archangel Chamuel	Known as the Peace Angel who can help you in love and relationships. This is the Angel to call upon when you need strength to move forward due to unexpected events in your finances or even relationships.
Archangel Barakiel	Known as the Good Fortune Angel who can help you view things as blessings rather than challenges. This is the Angel to call upon when you need guidance or to see with clarity in a monetary situation.

Archangel Gamaliel	Known as the Gift Giver Angel who can bring small or large gifts that you may not have expected. This can come in the form of others helping you, actual money, or even the gift of divine love in all areas of your life. This is the Angel to call upon when you are looking to increase your daily flow of abundance overall.
Archangel Gadiel	Known as the Wealth Angel who can help take your abundance to the next level in all areas of your life. This is the Angel to call upon when you are ready to elevate to the next level in your abundance flow.
Archangel Uriel	Known as the Knowledge Angel. This is the Angel to call upon when you need guidance, to seek clarity in your life, or even to demonstrate your knowledge.
Archangel Pathiel	Known as the Open Doors Angel who can help you expand your abundance by seeing new opportunities. This is the Angel to call upon when you are ready to diversify your income.

There are many Archangels that you can call upon, but these are the ones that are particularly assigned to help you with money matters. You can also call upon Archangel Michael and Gabriel for guidance and protection at all times.

Now that you are familiar with each of the Archangels, let's take a closer look at how you can connect with each of them.

Spiritual Practices on Connecting with the Archangels

The most common way that you can connect with the Archangels is through prayer. You have the option of creating your own Angel prayer, or you can ask the Spirit to guide you with this connection.

Depending on your spiritual origin, you may have an instant connection and they may be communicating with you already. If that is the case, then you can just call on them by name and they will come to you to assist you in whatever way you need.

Here's a prayer that I wrote in one of my Prayer Therapy courses back when I was working on becoming an Intuitive Life Coach and Spiritual Celebrant (Ordained Interfaith Minister).

"Lord, I don't know everything, but I am asking you to give me knowledge and wisdom to make the right choices to glorify you. You are my provider and my sole source for everything. Lord, you are more than enough for me. I surrender to your will for my life.

Open my Heart to Receive what you have in store for me. Teach me, Lord, so that I can move towards a more righteous path. In Jesus Name…Amen!"

I value teaching each of you how to connect to your own intuition and that's how I feel about prayer. This is your own unique spiritual journey and personal relationship with God. You owe it to yourself to learn how to communicate with God and the Angels beyond prayer, but also meditation. As I have learned through my own spiritual walk, God and the Angels will communicate with you, but you have to learn how to be still and listen. In the next chapter, I will discuss more about how to use your intuition and manifest using positive affirmations.

Chapter 8:

Using Your Intuition and Positive Affirmations to Manifest

In this chapter, you will:

- Learn what intuition is and why you need to know about yours.
- Describe the different types of intuition.
- Identify a resource on how to connect to your intuition.
- Apply positive affirmations to attract abundance.

What Is Intuition?

Humans have been born with the ability to use intuition for centuries. The history of psychology showcases many of the major thought leaders who focused on the body, mind, and spirit such as Descartes; but did not get the respect that they deserved because society did not see the value in intuition.

Therefore, over time, intuition has been suppressed in us, or undervalued because of the Church Movement. I teach people that both prayer and meditation are important to harness. Prayer is asking God to deliver something into your life. On the other hand, meditation is where God *instructs* or *shows you a vision* on *how* to move forward on your life path.

A lot of people don't know how to use their intuition because it was not always taught in the Church. We are now living in times where our faith and intuition is all we have to help navigate life situations and seize opportunities that appear on your path in divine timing. Intuition is how the Spirit communicates with you. You may have heard people say, "trust your gut," "I felt a churn in my stomach," or "I got an eerie feeling," "you must be psychic." All these phrases describe intuition. Every human being has the ability to connect *directly* with the Spirit but it does require spending time with God to deepen your personal relationship with Him. Let's take look at a few ways in which the Spirit can communicate with you depending upon your born identity.

Types of Intuition

There are seven types of intuition that can be used to communicate with God. In order to access your intuition, you have to develop your own personal relationship with the Spirit, God, the Great Divine, or whatever you call the source in your faith to see how the Spirit wants to communicate with you. I cannot stress to you how personal this experience with God is. Each individual's journey is different, and how you communicate with the Divine may be different than how someone else does.

Clairaudience

The first type of intuition is clairaudience, which is the ability to receive an intuitive vocal message from the world of spirits or a higher being. People with this gift can hear messages that may come in the form of particular words, names or phrases, audio, mini music clips, or unintelligible sounds that may be known to them and the Spirit. Clairaudience can also come through dreams as one may hear the voice of a spirit during sleep. For example, you may have a dream of your grandmother or other family member. If you are an intuitive who has this spiritual gift, then you hear straight from the Spirit. You don't need any tools to help you gain divine intelligence.

Clairsentient

The second type of intuition is clairsentience, which is the ability to have clear sense. If you ever met someone or have walked into a building and gotten a certain feeling, whether it was good or bad, that was your intuition letting you know the juice or the real deal. If you are gifted with this type of intuition, you may be able to feel the present, past, or future physical and emotional states of other people. Questions that can help you develop this spiritual gift are the following:

1. How do I feel when I am….?
2. Do I feel good or bad…?
3. When did this feeling occur…?

You may also say or hear other people talk about a gut feeling or a churn in their stomach. That's just a nice way of saying "intuitively" because intuition is an abstract topic like abstract math.

Empath

The third type of intuition is empath, which means people with this gift can feel emotions and energy. With this type of gift, one can intuit how people around them feel or even be able to assess an environment. If you are wondering if you have the abilities of an empath, then look into other esoteric and spirituality topics such as astrology and numerology. These can help you explore the depths of your life path as a spiritual being. You can do that by learning your sun sign, moon sign, and rising sign. It will give you key information about your life, habits, and future outlook. Chances are, if you are a water sign or have water in your chart then you feel emotions deeply and you may be considered an empath.

Clairvoyant

The fourth type of intuition is clairvoyance. Many religions associate it with the gift of prophecy. Intuition has been explored by early philosophers such as Descartes and others, especially during the Renaissance Period. The psychologist Freud claims that "energy is a Mind System," and it truly is as you begin to understand the self more and explore deeper parts of the soul and mind.

Individuals who are clairvoyant can see past, present, and future in the forms of mini-movies, visions, dreams, numbers, or however the Spirit/Great Divine/or whatever you call God in your faith chooses to communicate with you. No tools are necessary with this gift as it just happens naturally.

Claircognizant

The fifth type of intuition is claircognizance. This is the gift where you know something without understanding how you know it. It can come in the form of thoughts, messages from your intuition, or you understand a situation without needing to think about it. It's sort of like guessing the right answers to a math problem, but you can't explain how you got the answer.

Channeling

The sixth type of intuition is channeling. This type of intuition can be associated with Mediumship. Depending on the gift, Archangels, Ancestors, or other Spirits can contact someone who has this specific ability to share a message with you from the other side. You may see a lot of TV shows centered on this particular gift.

Spiritual Guide

The seventh type of intuition is Spiritual Guides. This type of intuition deals with your spiritual team. There are many types of spiritual guides who can provide advice and assistance in any situation, but you must ask.

For example, I work with the Archangels, Ascended Masters, and my Spiritual Guides and Guardian Angels. Spiritual Guides are positive energies that are here for your highest good and I teach people how to connect to their own. The first step is asking God and your spiritual team for support to learn how they want to communicate with you. It's in that process that you will learn your own unique spiritual gifts that can be shared with the World. That's the whole point of connecting to your intuition, but it does require faith.

The second step is to learn how to meditate as the Spirit communicates to you when your mind is quiet, and you are listening rather than asking. A lot of people focus only on prayer and prayer is needed, but that's you telling the Spirit what you need or want. The Spirit already knows what you need and want so you need to listen to the Spirit as well and be obedient to what the Spirit wants to share with you in order to navigate whatever situation you have going on.

I encourage you to test each Spirit that you come into contact with as your own intuition will guide you on whether you should proceed or not. That's where your intuition comes into play; to help you gain insights and knowledge to apply in your own life for self-discovery and spiritual growth. If the Spirit leads you, share with me your insights about your own intuition.

Positive Affirmations to Attract Abundance

You can attain abundance through positive affirmation. Your view of yourself plays a huge role to your success; therefore, it's important to affirm yourself. There are several ways you can do that, but I am a huge fan of positive affirmations because energy is a mind system. The more that you can reprogram your thoughts on a subconscious level, the easier it is to manifest and attract abundance or whatever you desire.

Below are some positive affirmations that you can write on sticky note or whatever you choose to do as it applies to your own heart's desires:

Positive Affirmations for Attracting Abundance
1. Gratitude-I am grateful. Be thankful for the far you have come as this fuel your desire to go further.
2. I can do it. Believe that you can do it and watch your dream come closer.
3. I have what it takes. Identify your positive attributes and work on building on them.
4. My dream waits.

5. I have the right mindset to realize my dream.
6. Abundance is within reach for me-Believe it and watch it happen.
7. I Am at my best to realize my dream-Believe it.
8. I have a contribution to make to the world through the abundance.
9. My efforts are not in vain.
10. I am good enough-Believe in yourself and affirm your strengths.
11. Dare to be different-Be willing to try out unchartered paths.
12. I choose positivity-A positive mindset is a strong driving force.
13. A lot depends on me-Believe it and act the part.
14. I realize my self-worth-It's important to know your value.
15. I choose happiness over fear-I override fear with confidence.
16. I believe in me- This is essential to attract abundance.
17. I am successful-I believe I will make it.
18. I am at peace with myself.
19. I receive what I give-giving is important.
20. I am a magnet to success.

In this chapter, we focused on learning what intuition is, how to use intuition, and positive affirmations to manifest. Now that you have some strategies to put in your toolbox, it's time to move on to the next step. Step four is about navigating the opportunities. The first task in learning how to navigate opportunities that come your way is to define success. Let's take a deeper look at some strategies on how to allow success to happen.

Step 4: Navigate the Opportunities

Chapter 9:
What is Success?

In this chapter, you will:
- Identify what is success.
- Define what success means to you.
- Explain the importance of doing your personal best.
- Learn strategies on how to allow success to happen.
- Describe why resistance is self-sabotage.
- Describe reasons why you cannot outsource your life's work.
- Analyze scenarios related to choosing divine love over the go.

What is Success and What Does It Mean To You?

Success can have different means to each person. In your own words, how would you define success? What does it mean to you?

Write your own definition here and share what it means to you:

_____
_____
_____
_____

Success is about you taking the time out to measure your goals that you have set for yourself. It doesn't mean that you are in competition with other people. You have to get to the point in knowing that you are in healthy competition with yourself and that's how you are going to define your success as you learn how to dominate in your field of study or industry by being your authentic self.

The Importance of Doing Your Personal Best

Work requires commitment and doing your best brings about success in your work. Working at peak performance requires a combination of steps for an effective system to promote great work.

There are several steps for you to do your personal best in work. First, you need to establish personal values. You will get skills for better decision making and can act under any circumstances if you do your best in work. You get the future you want by taking on the guiding light in your values. Informed decisions are made from realizing your goals and values.

Rehearse your work for a successful outcome. If you can visualize your work, it will increase efficiency and confidence overall. This way, when obstacles come, they will not get throw you off as you have a set picture of what you want in your work.

Did you know that the world needs your best work? Your work has your fingerprint on it, and only you can do it the way you do. When you do your personal best at work, you help make the world a better place.

Work is not easy; that's why it's a lot of work. During the times when you feel you cannot give it your best; it helps if you to remember this is the time to give it your best. The quality of the work you do reflects how much you care for your job.

People who care about their work pour themselves in it without holding anything back. It calls for hours of commitment and sacrifice at times but is well the effort from the results. In the end, hard work always pays, and if you give it your best, you will no doubt see the results in the end.

Strategies to Allow Success to Happen

Each of us has goals they'd like to fulfill in life. At times it might be a struggle to attain success in life, but we need to push through to allow it to happen. Having clear goals and wanting to achieve them may not be enough in itself but you also need to have the right strategies as well. You need to be consistent in the quest for success and be resilient for it to happen.

Here are four strategies you should have to realize success in life.

1. *Have a plan in place.* For you to realize your dreams you need to have a detailed plan in place. Not only that but you need to mule over it, and also work on it so as to achieve success. You should not stop until you achieve your hearts' desire for success.
2. *Self discipline.* This is essential to be able to realize success in your goals. With discipline even the most difficult tasks can be achieved while even simple tasks appear impossible where there is no discipline. Keep the right habits to allow you be self disciplined.
3. *Time management.* This is critical for you to enjoy success. Instead of wasting the time you have put it in good use in an effort to realize your goals. Separate urgent tasks from those that can wait and do not waste time in time wasting activities or dealing with interruptions to the plan you have in place.
4. *Get a mentor.* Find someone who has walked the path you are intent on taking. This helps during times when you come across difficulties in your walk to success. Like a ray of hope a mentor points you in the right direction offering hope in turbulent days. It helps for you to have someone shining light upon your path to success.

Why Resistance is Self-Sabotage?

You can sabotage success through resistance. Change is inevitable and refusing to accept it will curtail your chances of success. If you can have an open mind and embrace it, you'll are better placed to attain more in life.

Below are reasons why resistance is self-sabotage:

1. *Resistance stems from fear of the unknown.* You do not want to try out the new because you are not sure what lies ahead. If you are not willing to take a risk, you'll not achieve much in life. You can hardly achieve anything if you do not take a bold step towards your dreams.
2. *You are in a hurry to get there, and your impatience could cost you.* Did you know you could sabotage yourself by refusing to weigh your options? Take time to think things over and learn from others if you can. There are resources available to point you in the right direction, therefore, do not be resistant from new ideas.
3. *Some people fear criticism should things not work out as expected.* If you listen to the views of other people, you will hardly achieve anything. Resist taking them into account and believe in yourself. You have the ability to get things done, no doubt.
4. *Some people like to rationalize all that they do.* If it has to make sense for you to do it, you may not achieve a lot in life. Take the leap without going too much into

details of what you expect. It pays to believe that things will work out well in the end.
5. *Most times, we tend to tie our identity to success or lack of it.* Success or failure does not dictate who you are therefore let go of those disabling thoughts.

Why You Cannot Outsource Your Life's Work?

You are born for a purpose and you owe it to yourself to know what your divine life purpose is so that you can actively work towards the life lessons in which you are to learn to serve humanity. This is the primary reason why you cannot outsource your life's work because you are the overseer of your work. However, it is important to note that there are other souls who have agreed with you to take part of your life's work because it is also a part of their own life purpose as they move forward towards their own destiny. Therefore, it is so important to protect your life's work in every aspect. It is possible to hire other people to take care of your personal tasks. Your most basic chores included, and you can even get someone to take care of your emails as well. All with a goal to free up your time for more critical tasks. There are concerns when we outsource our lives work to other people, and here are some reasons you should not.

1. It can change one's sense of self in a couple of ways, making it difficult to connect with other people. In meeting our needs, we either do it ourselves while

involving the help of family and friends or pay someone to do it. Outsourcing breaks the connection with people close to us who would otherwise be involved in doing the work.
2. We lose the sense of community as the relationship with paid workers cannot come close to what we have close friends and family. Personal relationships suffer as a result as actual community bonds get formed when we get help and also help other people.
3. Outsourcing encourages specialization, which is doing what each person is good at doing. To be an all-rounded individual, you need to perform various tasks instead of concentrating on one of them.
4. Miss benefits we might have got along the way. They include cultivating character, self-confidence, and a sense of community and ownership of work. These are worthwhile lessons, especially for our children who then learn we must work for things as they do not work automatically.
5. Work is part of our lives. The more tasks we drop, the more we let go of parts of ourselves. Life is fulfilling when lived closest to its core; thus, we should not lose sight of the connection between results and effort.

The bottom line is that you should evaluate which aspects of your life's work that you can outsource, but it is important that you have written agreements in place to protect your life's work.

Chapter 10: Diversifying Your Income Potential

In this chapter, you will:
- Learn why diversifying your income is crucial.
- Describe streams of revenue that can bring wealth.
- Assess your skills and spiritual gifts to identify income potential.
- Learn life lessons from both the rich and poor.

Why Diversifying Your Income Is Important?

At times it can be challenging to survive on a regular income. You are multidimensional spiritual being so you have multiple intelligences that you should be using to carry out your divine life purpose. Over time, if you continue to work towards becoming a self-actualized person, you will learn that you have a plethora of skills and gifts that were bestowed upon you to utilize in this lifetime. Therefore, diversifying your income is important and it is natural to have more than one income source when you are utilizing all your God-given gifts and talents. With so many needs for extra cash, it becomes necessary to take on additional projects to bring in cash. There are various projects one can take, and they may not always be for the money that comes out of it. The experience you gain out of such might be worthwhile for your career in the end. You can take up part-time jobs to keep your career running. Say if you do not have a stable job, then you can do part-time jobs to keep you in tune with your career, and gain valuable experience at the same time.

Temporary jobs are those that are done for a while and do not bind you to the job. These, too, serve to help continuity between jobs and earn you cash as well. Instead of staying idle in between work, you can take on a seasonal job. They are mainly meant to fill in a temporary need and can help groom you for a stable position in the future.

You have more chances for networking if you take on these jobs. If you are eyeing big companies working as a temp is a great way for you to gain entry to them. If you portray your effectiveness while you are there, chances are you will get considered should it turn into a permanent position. When taking on extra projects, be sure to put in your best to have a more gainful experience. Whether it is extra cash you need, or you are after gaining experience and exposure in your career, these temporary assignments can be quite useful for you. There's nothing lost when you engage in any of them anytime.

Streams of Revenue to Accumulate Wealth

Do you think that you are a millionaire? What about a spiritual millionaire? Well, I am here to tell you that you have that potential in you. It takes a lot of work to become a millionaire and you must earn and invest money in more than one way to keep the dough rolling in. Millionaire status means that you must be committed to what you do and be excellent in what you do whatever that skillset may be. As I coach others to become the next Millionaire, I share with them that they have to make the choice first to accept wealth into their life. So, before we continue, answer the following question:

> Wealth Reflection: Do I want to be Wealthy? YES or NO

You may notice that I haven't asked you to explain why you want to be wealthy because that is not what this entire book has been about. The focus has been on helping you be in touch with your authentic self so that you can allow abundance and prosperity to flow in your life naturally. So, if you said Yes, then you have done a lot of the hard part. Now, you are going to allow messages and other guides help you on your life path towards accumulating wealth. We looked back at some industries earlier, but there are five main ways that people accumulate wealth and it may or may not be in those industries mentioned earlier. Below are the five ways that people can become wealthy:

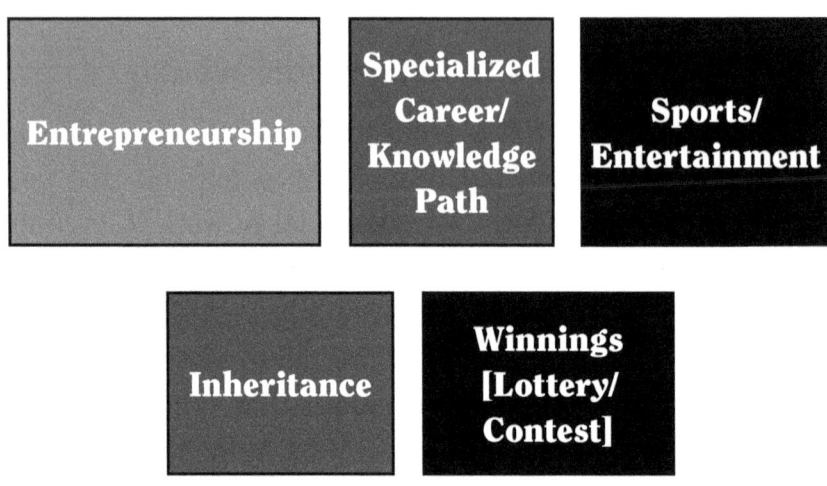

As you can see, millionaires have several revenue streams from which to draw. Millionaires do not depend on one source of income but tap into different resources for success. Below are some additional revenue streams of income that build millionaires:

1. *Investing in Stocks.* Stock investments will offer you passive income besides your primary source. You can buy stocks then wait for the value to appreciate before you sell them. They earn you money if you're able to predict the right time to sell them accurately.
2. *Earning Interest from Your Bank Accounts.* Keep money in the bank, and it will earn you interest with

time. There are types of bank accounts that make you cash if you leave your cash in there for some time. Let your money work for you as you engage in other sources of income in the meantime.
3. *Starting a Digital or Internet Business.* An internet-based business is a good investment and can turn your fortunes around in no time at all. You can sell your goods online or have an online shop to conduct your business. In a day when most people buy all kinds of stuff online, you can glean sales from an internet-based business.
4. *Become a Lender or Investor.* Lend your personal cash either to individuals or companies and earn interest on loans. There's little cost in such investment except for perhaps guarantee of security for the loans. Invest if you have the cash to spare and watch it grow with time. If you are serious about lending or investing, then look at your state's requirements to tap into the financial industry to support individuals and/or small businesses.
5. *Earning Income from Your Business.* Business income is your primary source of income. It could be passive such as a business that has other people running it and not you directly. The idea is for you to build one that generates income while giving you the necessary exposure for your skills.

If you are committed to generating income, there are many ideas into which you can tap. All of which can lead to becoming a millionaire in the long run. Now, let's take some time out to assess your skills and spiritual gifts to identify your income potential.

Assess Your Skills and Spiritual Gifts to Identify Income Potential

All money ain't good money. I learned this firsthand growing up in the hood and watching people lose their lives or go to jail behind a bid that was not even theirs. However, it became a part of their karma bill because they choose to accept payment for whatever they had agreed with. We call this in the spiritual world "energy exchange". We will discuss more about energy exchanges later in the last step of my framework, DAMNU. Before you can begin to create money the way that your soul wants to express itself, you will need to answer a few more questions. You did this in *Step 1: Discover Your Life Purpose*. Please go back to both Chapters one and two and take that information to use in this section. You will need the responses to fully help you see how you diversify your income potential. Please write down your answers to the following questions:

1. Out of the following industries, which ones are you interested in and why?
   A) Computer and Technology
   B) Health Care and Allied Health
   C) Education and Social Services
   D) Arts and Communications
   E) Trades and Transportation

F) Management, Business, and Finance
G) Architecture and Civil Engineering
H) Science
I) Hospitality, Tourism, and the Service Industry
J) Law and Law Enforcement

_____
_____
_____
_____
_____
_____
_____
_____
_____
_____
_____
_____
_____
_____

2. Taking the specific industries, you selected, what are some specific jobs that you can do? What are the educational/licensure requirements, if any?

_____
_____
_____
_____

3. What are your plans to move forward with gaining the proper paperwork to move forward with any of these selected careers?

_____
_____
_____
_____
_____

4. Where do you see yourself in 1-4 years in these chosen industries?

_____
_____
_____
_____
_____

These are four questions that are important to help you assess where you can use your talents and spiritual gifts. If you happen to have a criminal record, then these same strategies can apply to you too. From experience, God can use all his people, but it is important to first understand who you are and why you are here to design your life. No matter the mistake that you have made in your life, your position with God has not changed and for that reason, there is still hope if you keep the faith about your life purpose.

As you continue to be honest with yourself about who you are as a person, this will help improve your energy flow to attract opportunities that will allow you to move forward on your life path according to what God has ordained for you.

Now let's look at a few life lessons from the rich and the poor.

Life Lessons from Living in Poverty

One thing that I have learned from working with people from all walks of life is that it's not about where you live, what you do, where you work, or who you hang out with. It has everything to do with your integrity and your character. I have seen so many people part ways with their money for one reason or another because they were out of alignment with what God had called them to do for their life purpose. Issues related to the ego got the best of them and it affected their abundance and prosperity because they did not learn their life lessons or took their life role for granted. Any life situation you find yourself in can be a learning platform for you. You can learn some useful lessons living in poverty just like with any other situation. These are some life lessons that I learned while living in poverty and I still use them today because I no longer associate myself as either being in poverty or rich. That's limiting and that's not how God sees us. We are more than enough, and we have the limitless power to attract abundance and prosperity. It's our divine birthright.

Here are some money lessons you can learn when living in poverty:

1. *Make what you have run longer.* It might involve shopping around for bargain prices. You can make some things at home, such as soap to cut back on the cost of purchasing them. Look out for double coupon days in stores as well.
2. *It's expensive to be poor.* Most of the time, one gets forced to buy in small quantities, which ends being more costly in the long run. Getting cut off from utilities will cost you to have them reconnected as well, making it more expensive than if you were able to pay for them on time.
3. *There are plenty of ways for you to make money.* You will find many things you can do for money when living in poverty. As long as you are not afraid to get your hands dirty, there's always something you can do for a little upkeep. Just keep your eyes open to opportunities around you.
4. *It's okay to accept help.* We all want to be self-reliant, but at times it may not be possible when living in poverty. Accept help when you need it, as it may help carry you through the rough days. Poverty will pass, and you can get an opportunity to give to other people as well.
5. *Poverty teaches you the value of things.* You do not take what you have for granted, as you know how it

feels to be without it. This is one of the greatest lessons you can carry through the rest of your life.

Life Lessons from Being Rich

Being rich is a state of mind. However, wealthy is a different story. If you ask any wealthy person, they will tell you there are money lessons they learned by being rich. These lessons come from earning their wealth. Here are a few of the life lessons that I learned from the Rich:

1. *Money is not always the driving force.* At times one can start purely from passion, as was the case with some of the most famous people we know. Most of them relied on passion for spurring them on even in the most discouraging times.
2. *It's okay to take a risk.* You do not have to know the outcome of what you set to do but should be fine getting out of your comfort zone. Many rich people got where they are by taking chances with opportunities they discovered. There can be no certainty when building wealth, and all you have to do is work hard at what you set your heart on.
3. *Self-discipline is a requirement.* Most people begin to buy stuff when the money starts to trickle in without putting some into savings. Set some goals regarding your money and maintain discipline as far as it is concerned. If you fall into impulsive buying, you could easily miss the mark.

4. *Assets and income.* Note the difference between the two. While income stays until retirement but assets continue to generate income well after one has retired. Use your income to buy assets for a secure retirement.
5. *There are no shortcuts to wealth but to work hard.* Forget about winning the lottery or hoping to fall into an inheritance; wealth comes from hard work. You cannot afford to procrastinate and hope to get wealthy; therefore, you should be ready to put in many hours of work to realize success. Many wealthy people put in well over 50 hours a week to sustain their business. Therefore, they will not waste their time on tasks that do not generate revenue. That's why it is so important to have a healthy balance on what money really is because the wrong idea can have one focused on the wrong outcome. The outcome should be to make a profit if it is a business, but it should be done with integrity and positive intentions to continue to attract the energy that is necessary to serve humanity.

You have learned how to navigate the opportunities from Step Four of the Dr. Holland's DAMNU framework. Now, let's look at the last step, which is Step Five: *Utilize Your God-Given Talents.* You need to know what to do when you have money!

Step 5: Utilize Your God-Given Talents

Chapter 11:
Honoring Your Value and Worth

In this chapter, you will:
- Learn why it is important to honor your value and worth.
- Learn why it is more important to feel emotionally secure.
- Evaluate why you are making career and job changes.
- Learn why lack of money doesn't rule your life purpose.

Why It Is Important to Honor Your Value and Worth

As you learned at the beginning of this book in Step one, it is extremely important to honor your value and worth. Over time, you will learn that opportunities come and go and the people that you thought had your back never did. You were always responsible for yourself and your actions, behaviors, and choices. Depending on how much you valued yourself, you taught people how to treat you. This does not change if you earn more income. You still must honor and value yourself because no one else will. This is a hard reality that you will have to come to terms with at some point of your life to fully understand your place in this World. You are working with others and they have agreed on a spiritual level to help you meet your life purpose. This is true because part of their life purpose is to help you at either various parts of your life's work or throughout your life's work.

Why It is Important to Feel Emotionally Secure

It is more important to feel emotionally secure than focus solely on financial wealth. Wealth comes with many responsibilities, which can affect one's sense of happiness. If you target having more money, you could compromise your relationships in the end. There are things that money cannot buy you, and one of them is happiness. Dwell on your relationships with people as they will afford you security more than wealth. What I know about divine love, it heals and prospers you. Therefore, if you are manifesting healthy relationships in your personal and professional life, then you will be able to increase your abundance. It's one thing to continue dealing in situations where you know they are toxic and no real love is present, but a totally different one when you are learning how to navigate relationships through spiritual eyes. Make no mistake, we need money to survive, but money should be looked at from a healthy viewpoint. In other words, money should be considered as a tool to carry out the tasks that are necessary for your life purpose. If you are not connected to your life purpose, then you will mismanage your money on things that do not move you closer to your destiny. It is common sense to save cash for a rainy day. While this cushion you against emergencies affording your financial security, you must spend some money on yourself as well. Be kind to yourself and use some of the money you make to make yourself happy. You will realize having cash stacked in the bank does little to reinforce emotional security you experience from relationships with other people. The harsh reality is that you cannot take money with you when you transition to the afterlife, but you can take divine love with you in your heart and soul.

There is security in new experiences; therefore, spend some money in pleasurable experiences as it magnifies the way we view things giving a broader perspective. Experiences we have last longer since there are feelings attached to them. Instead of merely spending cash, invest in adventures as they give you secure feelings. Being secure in yourself stops you from comparing yourself with other people. Avoid measuring yourself against other people as each person has his abilities at the end of the day. Manage your expectations, so you do not end up feeling inadequate at the end of the day. Your sense of wellbeing comes from being able to manage your finances properly. There's no disputing the fact that financial wealth offers security, but that's not to say you should neglect personal relationships that caters to your emotional body and spirit. You have more emotionally security to gain from them than stashing vast amounts of cash in the bank. Remember, you are a spiritual being having human experiences and that's why emotional security is worth more than silver and gold.

Look Closer At Why You Are Changing Jobs or Careers

There are several questions you should ask yourself if you intend to make a job change. You don't want to make a move that will cost you much more later; therefore, ask yourself these few questions before you do. These questions are also designed to help you grow spiritually as that is one of the primary reasons of why you are working in the first place as you continue to grow in your chosen life path.

1. **What is the long-term effect of the job change?** Consider the impact this will have on your resume. It will not help for you to get viewed as a job hopper by future employers; therefore, think about the impact it will have on your reputation.
2. **How does the new job compare to the old one?** You will not find a perfect job anywhere. However, it is important to consider the pros and cons before deciding. Which of the two jobs take you closer to your goals? It will help you better decide.

3. **How about my connections?** In today's world, connections matter a lot, and building a network can take quite some time. Consider the people you are going to leave behind and decide if your new job is worth all the compromise, you will have to make.
4. **Will I be able to grow at my new job?** This is an important question to ask yourself to help you decide if to make the switch. No one likes to get stuck at one point on the job; therefore, find out if there's potential for advancement in your new job.
5. **What does my intuition say?** Listening to your sixth sense could determine what kind of decision you are going to make. Your gut feeling can save you from future trouble. The decision could affect the rest of your life; therefore, it should not be made in a rush. Listen to your gut feeling, pay heed to what it says.

Now, let's look at why the lack of money doesn't rule your life purpose.

Why Lack of Money Doesn't Rule Your Life Purpose

Purpose births your dreams. It doesn't matter if you don't have money; if you have a life purpose, you will no doubt pull through. If you discover your life purpose, you'll be happier doing what you do and can even make more wealth. It makes a difference in your financial life. I know from experience on my own journey that God will provide you the people, places, and things to move you forward towards your life purpose.

The only thing that you need is your faith because it activates what God wants to do in your life for you and through you. The next task is to do the work because faith without works is dead. You can't ask God to help you, if you don't help yourself towards your own life purpose. Even if you don't have the money to work on certain tasks, you can always look for other alternatives to work around that task and focus on what you can without the funds until God shows you a solution through your intuition. That's why your intuition is so important as you are navigating opportunities and other areas of your life.

Finding your life meaning serves as inspiration for developing better financial habits. If you can find the thing that makes you feel happy and fulfilled, makes your days' worth living, and inspires you to get out of bed each day, you have found your life purpose. It doesn't cost anything, but it gives you more fulfillment than even money will. You don't need to have money to find your life purpose as it can stem out of, say, service to other people.

Since it comes from within, it is therefore not dictated by other people but is a decision made on your own. Your life purpose is mainly driven by love and gives you fulfillment from pursuing your path in life. Since money is not the overriding factor in your life purpose, lack of it will not derail you whatsoever. You can get on with it in the absence of finances since that is not what inspires you. It is not the reward that comes from doing what you love doing but the satisfaction in knowing you were able to pull through with it. Your life purpose could be helping the poor around the world or saving the environment, whatever it is, you can be sure of making it since you possess the drive in you. Money is not the main factor but could only come in as a secondary result of your purpose in life.

At the end of the day, you owe it to yourself to continue to honor yourself and value your connections as you learn how to give and receive divine love in all areas of your life. In the next chapter, we will look at what it means to have money. Additionally, we will look at strategies that will help you learn how to save and make your money work for you. Remember, you are a King and Queen of the Most High and it is important that you know how to be good stewards of the material possessions that God has called you to oversee as you serve others in whatever capacity God has called you to lead.

Chapter 12:
Having Money

In this chapter, you will:
- Differentiate having money vs. financial wealth.
- Describe why saving money is important.
- Creating SMART financial goals.
- Identifying your personal values for your finances.
- Creating a personal finance plan that supports your beliefs.
- Learn the purpose of intentions in gift-giving and serving others.
- Learn the secrets about investing money.

Money vs. Financial Wealth

Having money is being able to take care of your basic needs and there is a steady income flow that comes in whether it is weekly, bi-weekly, monthly, or per project.

This is a good situation to be in and you should be able to monitor how you are spending your money so that you can meet your basic needs and even save money. On the other hand, financial wealth is having more than enough to where you are able to meet your basic needs, save, and invest your money in other people, causes, and projects. Depending on where you are in your life's journey, it will depend on what you need to do with the positive cashflow that comes in. In either case, you have money, but it boils down to what you do with that money that truly matters the most. If you are not careful, you can go broke in either money situation. Let's take a look at why saving money is important.

Why Saving Money is Important?

Saving money is a no brainer. Putting away some cash for a rainy day is worth it. You have peace of mind knowing you have money stashed away for a rainy day. Make a habit of saving some of the money you make and accumulate your savings.

Having savings in the right places, you can watch your money work for you. You will put in less work overtime and might even be able to stop working altogether.

At the time, when you enjoy an abundance of purpose to save some cash for the days, you may not have anything to put away. There's no better time for you to save than when you have some money to spare; therefore, do not hesitate to go ahead, do it.

You can never be sure about the future and need cash to fall back on in case of an emergency. Saving money keeps you from taking loans to take care of emerging needs that cannot wait; therefore, it should be a priority.

The money will never be enough, but it is a worthwhile endeavor for you to keep away some for later use. There's no better time than during times of abundance for you to make savings. It might be during the high season in your business or when you do not have too many financial commitments chipping away at your finances, but go ahead, save some cash. You never know when you'll need it, and the money you save could help you invest in further business.

It may surprise you the amount of cash you can save by keeping away small amounts of cash each time you receive some. It will add on to your savings no matter the amount you put in there.

Times of abundance serve as the best time for you to save some cash since you have a lot of money coming in.

Creating SMART Financial Goals

You may have heard of SMART goals in school or at some point during your life. Well, you also have to set SMART goals that are *specific, measurable, achievable, realistic, and timely*. It is important that you stick to each of these attributes when setting your goals because you want to see some progress in a specific timeframe. You might face self-doubt and distractions may get in the way but stay firm of the financial vision that you have set out for yourself.

So, let's look at an example of a SMART Financial Goal:

- *I will completely eliminate my $3,000 credit card debt and achieve a greater degree of financial security within three years by using 15% of each paycheck to pay the cards off.*

In this example, the key thing to recognize is that it is a specific dollar amount, percentage of paycheck, and a specific timeframe. You may notice that I didn't specify a specific credit card debt because this may apply to one specific credit card or overall credit card debt. This could be broken down further to gain more clarity.

Here are a few more examples to show you how this process works:

1. *I will buy myself the luxury model car I've always wanted by saving 8% each month for the next two years so I'll have a $5,500 down payment.*
2. *I will save enough money to cover six months' worth of expenses to use in case of emergencies by February 2021.*
3. *I will save for the ceiling fan project by saving $500 to pay for a new fan in each room in the next six months by putting aside 12% of our income.*

Now that you have reviewed some examples, it is time for you to write some of your own SMART financial goals.

Here's some space to write your goals:

Goal #1
S _____
M _____
A _____
R _____
T _____

Goal #2
S _____
M _____
A _____
R _____
T _____

Goal #3
S _____
M _____
A _____
R _____
T _____

Goal #4
S _____
M _____
A _____
R _____
T _____

Goal #5
S _____
M _____
A _____
R _____
T _____

Self-Reflection

Will I Be Wealthy or Wise? What is your decision? Explain.

_____
_____
_____
_____
_____

Now that you have taken the time out to self-reflect upon this question, it is time for you to identify your personal values for your finances so that you can move forward with the goals in which you have set out for your financial present and future.

Identifying Your Personal Values for Your Finances

The first step in creating a personal finance plan is to make sure that it supports or aligns with your beliefs. If you do not do that, then you can definitely believe that your spending habits will reveal to you what you belief in and teach you tough life lessons as you learn how to have a better relationship with your money.

Here are some questions to help you identify and assess whether your personal values are in alignment with your financial goals:

1. Why am I buying this? What purpose does it serve? Is it a short-term or long-term purpose?

   _____
   _____
   _____
   _____
   _____

2. How can I use this purchase six months down the road? What about one year?

   _____
   _____
   _____
   _____
   _____

3. Am I getting closer to my financial goals with this purchase decision? Why or why not?

   _____
   _____
   _____
   _____
   _____

4. How do I feel after making this purchase?

5. Is this feeling based upon my material needs or spiritual needs? How do I know?

6. Are you happy with what you bought? Did the feeling last? Why or why not?

7. What is the opportunity cost of this purchase?

Each of these questions can help you with a one-time purchase, short-term, or major purchase. As you program your mind to think about every purchase, it will help you get better at deciding on whether you need to make a purchase immediately or not. For instance, if you are making purchases based upon feelings, then this will help you identify if the feelings are fear-based or out of love-based. In other words, you want to make sure that you have thoroughly justified your purchase based upon your deepest needs. This will allow you to reprogram your mind towards making better choices in how you decide to use your money as you continue to refine your personal finance system.

Creating a Personal Finance Plan

The next step is to create a personal finance plan. This is a plan where you need to have a budget in place that goes beyond the necessities. When setting a budget, you need to ensure that your income covers your expenses. The rule of the thumb is to consider your priorities, goals and preferences. Setting a budget and sticking to it helps you achieve your financial goals in the end. On the next page, there are some key reminders that you need to know to get ahead financially.

> **Reminder #1: Live within your Means.**

> **Reminder #2: Pay off Your Credit Cards.**

> **Reminder #3: Maintain an Emergency Fund.**

> **Reminder #4: Save for Retirement and Future Expenses.**

The first step is to have a budgeting plan in place. Your budget should cover your needs such as gas and groceries and your wants, such as a new wardrobe or accessories. You also need to save some cash for future use or to take care of any emergencies that might arise. Long term saving goals should also be considered in your budget. The number of saving accounts in which you have should match your savings goals. For example, if you are looking to save for a car, then you should have a savings account that is exclusively for the future car purchase, along with the regular savings account for your overall savings goals.

You'll be able to control your expenditure better and cut back on spending if you have a budget in place. The key is to set some cash to the side so that you can pay off debts. Should you run low on your budget, you can cut back on some things such as entertainment to be able to pay your debts.

Set financial goals so you can tailor your budget around them. You'll be able to know where to focus your efforts, and you can decide how much to allocate for each goal. For instance, development goals are essential than entertainment; therefore, should take precedence between the two. Whatever you do, it is important that you are living within your means. Don't worry about what your friends think or what anybody else is doing because your budget is personal to you and your family. That's why it is called a *personal* finance system as it is unique to your financial situation.

Assigning Percentages in Your Budget

When it comes to assigning percentages in your budget, you want to make sure that you have a budget that is going to cover a range of your needs. Let's look at some of these percentages for a sample budget on the next page.

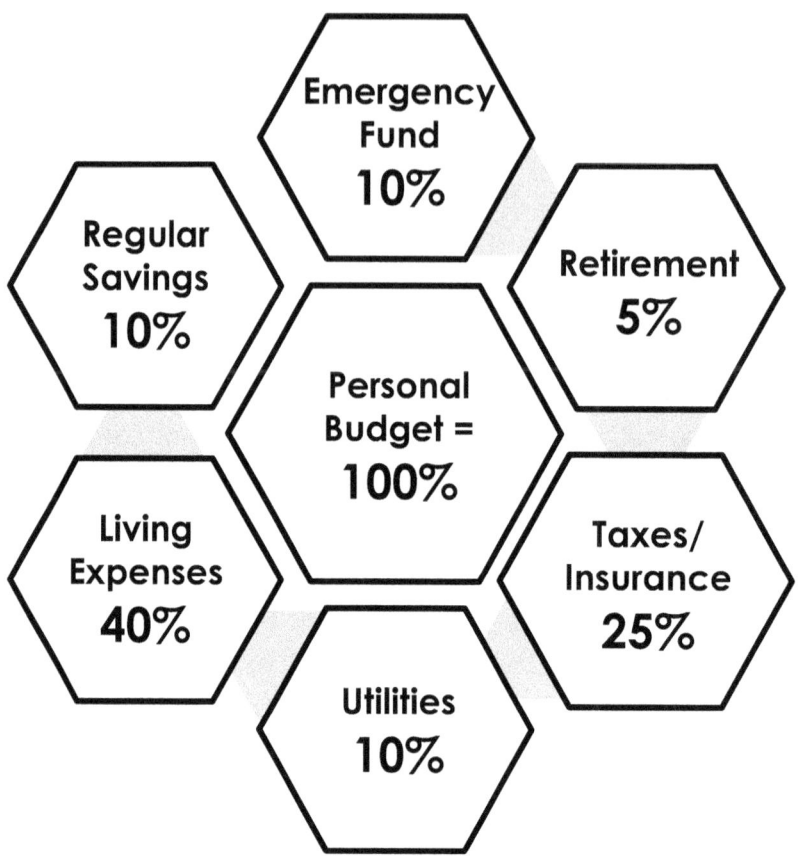

Please understand that this is an example of a way to assign budgets. Now, let's look at how these percentages translate into your spending plan. You need to think about your spending plan because it is the only way that you are going to be able to determine where your money is going and what is coming in. On the next page, there is a sample budgeting activity that you can use as a template to take control of your spending and overall finances each month.

BUDGETING ACTIVITY #1: *Taking a Deeper Look at Your Income in Your Spending Plan*

Income	What Coming in for the Month?	What Do You Want Your Monthly Income To Be?
Income Source #1		
Income Source #2		
Income Source #3		
Income Source #4		
Investments		
Total Montly Income		

Here are some reflective questions to help you digest your income that is coming in and where you want to take it next:

1. What types of income do I have coming in? Are you happy with how much you are bringing in each month? Why or why not?

_____
_____
_____
_____

2. What do you want your monthly income to be? What is the purpose behind it beyond the fact that you want to earn more money each month?

_____
_____
_____
_____
_____

Now that you have documented your income and wrote down your heart's desires on what you want your monthly income to be, let's take a deeper look at your monthly expenses through several budgeting activities.

BUDGETING ACTIVITY #2: *Taking a Deeper Look at Your Living Expenses in Your Spending Plan*

Category: Living Expenses	What Are You Spending Each Month?	What Do You Want Your Monthly Expense To Be for this Category?
Mortgage or Rent		
Real Estate Taxes		
Home repairs/ maintenance		

Home Improvements		
Land Lease Rent (if applicable)		
HOA dues		
Home Needs (household items)		

Here are some reflective questions to help you assess your living expenses:

1. Are you happy with how much you are spending for this category in each month? Why or why not?

    _____
    _____
    _____
    _____
    _____

2. Where are some areas in this category that you can minimize your living expenses? What steps would you need to take?

    _____
    _____
    _____
    _____
    _____

Budgeting Activity #3: *Taking a Deeper Look at Your Utilities in Your Spending Plan*

Category: Utility Expenses	What Are You Spending Each Month?	What Do You Want Your Monthly Expense To Be for this Category?
Electric Bill		
Gas/Propane		
Water/Sewer		
Trash		
Phone (all phones)		
Internet		

Here are some reflective questions to help you assess your utilities expenses:

1. Are you happy with how much you are spending for this category in each month? Why or why not?

   _____
   _____
   _____
   _____

2. Where are some areas in this category that you can minimize your utility expenses? What steps would you need to take?

_____
_____
_____
_____
_____

Budgeting Activity #4: *Taking a Deeper Look at Your Food in Your Spending Plan*

I want you to get in the habit of breaking down your food expenses throughout the day and then the week to get an idea of what you are spending per meal, per day, per week, and overall, per month. You may or may not have all of these food expenses but use it according to how you spend in this category.

Category: Food Expenses	What Are You Spending Each Month?	What Do You Want Your Monthly Expense To Be for this Category?
Groceries		
Breakfast Eating Out		
Coffee/Tea Runs		

Lunch Eating Out		
Dinner Eating Out		
Family Eating Out		
Delivery Expenses		

Here are some reflective questions to help you assess your food expenses:

1. Are you happy with how much you are spending for this category in each month? Why or why not?

   _____
   _____
   _____
   _____
   _____

2. Where are some areas in this category that you can minimize your food expenses? What steps would you need to take?

   _____
   _____
   _____
   _____
   _____

Budgeting Activity #5: *Taking a Deeper Look at Your Transportation in Your Spending Plan*

Category: Transportation Expenses	What Are You Spending Each Month?	What Do You Want Your Monthly Expense To Be for this Category?
Vehicle Payment #1		
Vehicle Payment #2		
Gas		
Routine Auto Fees (Licenses/Stickers)		
Vehicle Repair Bill		
Public Transportation		
Rideshare/Taxis Expenses		
Air Fare		

Here are some reflective questions to help you assess your transportation expenses:

1. Are you happy with how much you are spending for this category in each month? Why or why not?

_____
_____
_____
_____

2. Where are some areas in this category that you can minimize your transportation expenses? What steps would you need to take?

___

Budgeting Activity #6: *Taking a Deeper Look at Your Insurances/Taxes in Your Spending Plan*

Category: Insurances/Taxes	What Are You Spending Each Month?	What Do You Want Your Monthly Expense To Be for this Category?
Auto Insurance		
Dental Insurance		
Healthcare Insurance		
Vision Insurance		
Life Insurance		
Home/Renter Insurance		
Membership Insurance #1		

Membership Insurance #2		
Income Taxes		
Business Taxes		
Miscellaneous Taxes		

Here are some reflective questions to help you assess your insurances/taxes expenses:

1. Are you happy with how much you are spending for this category in each month? Why or why not?

   _____
   _____
   _____
   _____

2. Where are some areas in this category that you can minimize your insurances/taxes expenses? What steps would you need to take?

   _____
   _____
   _____
   _____

Budgeting Activity #7: *Taking a Deeper Look at Your Savings in Your Spending Plan*

Category: Savings	What Are You Savings Each Month?	What Do You Want Your Monthly Savings To Be for this Category?
Emergency Funds		
Retirement #1		
Retirement #2		
Regular Savings		
Savings #1		
Savings #2		
Savings #3		

Here are some reflective questions to help you assess your savings expenses:

1. Are you happy with how much you are saving for this category in each month? Why or why not?

_____
_____
_____
_____

2. Where are some areas in this category that you adjust to save more of your money each month? What steps would you need to take?

_____
_____
_____
_____
_____

Budgeting Activity #8: *Taking a Deeper Look at Your Miscellaneous Expenses in Your Spending Plan*

Category: Miscellaneous Expenses	What Are You Spending Each Month?	What Do You Want Your Monthly Expense To Be for this Category?
Childcare Expenses		
Education Expenses		
Beauty Expenses		
Entertainment		
Bars/Date Nights		
Career Expenses		
Vacation Expenses		

Work Clothing Expenses		
Gym/Fitness Expenses		
Other Expense #1		
Other Expense #2		

Here are some reflective questions to help you assess your miscellaneous expenses:

1. Are you happy with how much you are spending for this category in each month? Why or why not?

   _____
   _____
   _____
   _____
   _____

2. Where are some areas in this category that you can minimize your miscellaneous expenses? What steps would you need to take?

   _____
   _____
   _____
   _____
   _____

Keep tracking your spending to help you adjust and keep you within your goals. For instance, set aside time to go through your weekly expenses to avoid losing track. More extended periods can turn out to be more challenging to manage. At the end of the day, you need to make sure that your spending plan is in alignment with your belief system so that you can honor yourself and continue with the financial goals in which you have set out for yourself and/or your family.

The Purpose Behind Gift-Giving and Serving Others

Gift-giving is a beautiful thing when it is given with positive intentions. It's natural when you are in leadership to serve others. However, just like all money ain't good money, the same concept applies to gifts—not every gift is meant to be taken. If you have to get it, then donate it to another cause as you are learning how to keep the flow of abundance going and completing the cycle of giving and receiving. There are different reasons for which gifts are given. At times you should not accept a gift given to you for various reasons. Gifts are meant to build relationships, therefore, consider turning down the ones you don't really want.

Here are some reasons you should not accept such gifts:

1) The gift might have a hidden meaning. While it is normal for your boss to give you a gift at the end of year party to appreciate your input at work, it might seem

odd if he keeps sending expensive gifts to you. It might be a way of making sexual advances to you.
2) In the corporate setting, receiving gifts from clients might go against the policies of the company. To avoid conflict of interest, desist from accepting any such gifts.
3) A gift can be used as a means of control if given by a person with whom you are in a relationship. Should the relationship fail to work out the giver can use the gift to continue contacting you even after you no longer desire anything of the sort.
4) You don't have to accept gifts from people you are not very close to on your special occasions. Say, for instance, on your Anniversary, anyone who's not a relative does not have to buy you a gift. You can politely decline such gifts.
5) At times people to go great lengths buying gifts they cannot afford. If someone offers you a gift which has you feeling that they sacrificed too much to buy it, you can decline. There's no need accepting something then get riddled with feelings of guilt after that.

Gifts are a good way of building relationships, but care should be taken on once you decide to accept them.

Learning to Invest Money Wisely

When it comes to investing money, there are some secrets that you should know to ensure that your money is continuing to work for you. I won't spend time teaching you on the various ways on how you need to invest your money because there are many books on the market to teach you how to participate in the stock market, become an investor in another business venture, buy gold, and etc. My role is to teach you about the purpose of investing and why you should continue to keep your money working for you wisely.

Money is an Energy

The first spiritual principle is that you need to understand that money is an energy. It is meant to continue to flow like a river and that's what you need to do. I have heard countless stories where people have stored up their money and didn't get a chance to use it because they either died or lost their money for one reason or another. When I began to look at these stories, then that's when I learned that it was about the flow of the energy of how that money was obtained.

Positive Intentions with Your Money

The second spiritual principle is that you will part ways with your money if your intentions are not pure and positive. Let me share a few bible verses with you to make this point and for you to pray and meditate to gain clarity on how you need to be setting your intention with your money. Below are these bible verses:

- ✓ *Hebrews 13:5: Keep your life free from love of money, and be content with what you have, for he has said, "I will never leave you nor forsake you".*

- ✓ *Proverbs 13:11: Wealth gained hastily will dwindle; but whoever gathers little by little will increase it*
- ✓ *Matthews 6:24: No one can serve two masters, for either he will hate the one and love the other, or he will be devoted to the one and despise the other. You cannot serve God and money.*
- ✓ *Proverbs 22:7: The rich rules over the poor, and the borrower is the slave of the lender.*
- ✓ *Proverbs 16:9: The heart of man plans his way, but the Lord establishes his steps.*
- ✓ *Proverbs 13:22: A good man leaves an inheritance to his children's children, but the sinner's wealth is laid up for the righteous.*
- ✓ *1 Timothy 5:8: But if anyone does not provide for his relatives, and especially for members of his household, he has denied the faith and is worse than an unbeliever.*

These are all good sacred texts to help you move forward in your relationship with your finances. If you get a feeling of when you are investing your money that doesn't feel right, then honor it. You owe it to yourself to investigate where that feeling is coming from because money is energy. This could be a tell-tale sign from your intuition that you need to rethink your decision about your investments. It could be that it may not be the right time to invest or the investment may not be in alignment with your life purpose.

Wise Investments with Your Money

The last spiritual principle that you need to be aware of is making sure that your investments are aligned with your personal belief system and that your investments align with your life purpose. When you are investing in your own projects, then it allows you to increase your abundance because you are still on your life path and moving forward on your spiritual journey. This type of decision will bring positive growth to your finances because you are doing the work that will attract more opportunities that are meant for you on your life path.

Another example is that you may decide to invest in other people and their projects. This is what you are supposed to be doing to serve humanity. If you are planning to do that, then you need to make sure that the business or projects are in alignment with your divine life purpose so that the investment can be fruitful for all parties involved. This is where your intuition comes in to play because it will guide you on whether you need to invest into that opportunity or not. It's not necessary for the business to be thriving already, but most investors will invest in opportunities that are already booming or have an established business plan.

These are three spiritual principles that will help you determine if you are making a wise investment with your money. It's important to reflect on these and use your intuition to make an informed decision in which can provide both spiritual and emotional growth.

Where to Go From Here

You can check out the Alise Spiritual Healing & Wellness Center to see how to schedule a creative strategy session, intuitive reading, life coaching session, flower essence session, or just to hang out and learn what we are all about. One of our coaches would be more than willing to support you with your goals. Our website is the following: www.alisehealingcenter.com

Looking for a guest speaker? Dr. Alise is available for speaking engagements.

Should you have questions or comments for us, suggestions for future material or tips, feel free to email us at support@alisehealingcenter.com.

You can also tune in to my radio show, The Alise Intuition Radio Show on all major digital podcast platforms. If you are interested in being a guest on the show, then use the aforementioned email address.

Class Tours and Conferences

Throughout the year, you can find me on one of my class tours and/or at one of our conferences. For more information. You can visit the Alise Spiritual Healing & Wellness Center's website to check upcoming events at www.alisehealingcenter.com or email us at support@alisehealingcenter.com to be added to our mailing list or inquiry about our events.

Notes

Notes

Notes

Notes

Notes

Notes

Notes

Notes

Notes

Notes

Notes

Notes

Notes

www.ingramcontent.com/pod-product-compliance
Lightning Source LLC
Chambersburg PA
CBHW070640050426
42451CB00008B/246